Contemporary Trends in Trade-Based Money Laundering

1st Edition, February 2024

D R N A N A K O J O O D I

authorHOUSE

AuthorHouse™
1663 Liberty Drive
Bloomington, IN 47403
www.authorhouse.com
Phone: 833-262-8899

Published by AuthorHouse 02/20/2024

ISBN: 979-8-8230-2208-8 (sc)
ISBN: 979-8-8230-2207-1 (e)

Library of Congress Control Number: 2024903483

Print information available on the last page.

Any people depicted in stock imagery provided by Getty Images are models, and such images are being used for illustrative purposes only.
Certain stock imagery © Getty Images.

This book is printed on acid-free paper.

Because of the dynamic nature of the Internet, any web addresses or links contained in this book may have changed since publication and may no longer be valid. The views expressed in this work are solely those of the author and do not necessarily reflect the views of the publisher, and the publisher hereby disclaims any responsibility for them.

ACKNOWLEDGEMENTS

I am highly grateful to the following individuals whose encouragement and support made the completion of this book possible. Their contributions have left an indelible mark on this project.

First and foremost, I extend my utmost gratitude to my nuclear family, especially my wife (Victoria Abena Takyi) for their unwavering support and understanding during the countless hours spent researching and writing. Your encouragement was pivoting for this endeavor.

Special thanks to my brother, Dr Francis Takyi for engaging in stimulating discussions and providing valuable feedback that helped shape the ideas presented in these pages. Your intellectual contributions were instrumental in refining the concepts explored in this book.

Finally, I want to express my gratitude to all my friends and colleagues who offered words of encouragement and moral support during this process. Your belief in the significance of this project provided the motivation needed to see it through to completion.

This book stands as a testament to the collective effort of these individuals, and I am sincerely thankful for their contributions to its completion.

Dr Philip Takyi
DBA, MABR, MBA, DF. CFIAG, FCILG, MIODs, FICA

ABSTRACT

Contemporary Trends in Global Trade-Based Money Laundering is a consolidated enlightenment of the advanced world of **illicit financial activities**, with a particular focus on the insidious phenomenon of **trade-based money laundering** (TBML). This book delves into complex mechanisms employed by perpetrators to exploit legitimate international trade transactions for the purpose of disguising the illicit origins of funds.

The narrative unfolds against the backdrop of a rapidly evolving global economy, where the financial ecosystems have provided both opportunities and challenges for those seeking to manipulate the financial landscape. Through meticulous secondary research and case studies, this book aims to demystify the methods employed in TBML, illuminating the various disguises, trade structures, and financial instruments utilized by money launderers.

Readers will embark on a journey through real-world examples of TBML, exploring high-profile cases that have characterized regulatory responses and law enforcement strategies. The book also provides an in-depth analysis of the gaps within existing international trade frameworks and financial systems that contribute to the success of TBML schemes.

The book further seeks to contribute to the ongoing discourse on anti-money laundering efforts, urging stakeholders to collaborate in creating a more robust and resilient financial ecosystem that upholds the principles of transparency, integrity, and accountability. In addition to showcasing the dynamics of TBML, the study offers a forward-looking perspective, proposing innovative solutions and policy recommendations aimed at fostering the resilience of the global financial system against the ever-evolving tactics of money launderers.

As the global community confronts the challenges posed by illicit financial activities, this book serves as a call to action, advocating for a united front against the shadowy forces that seek to undermine the integrity of international trade and finance.

CONTENTS

LIST OF FIGURES

LIST OF ACRONYMS

AML/CFT: Anti-money Laundering/Countering the Financing of Terrorism

APG: Asia Pacific Group on Money Laundering

BMPE: Black Market Peso Exchange

BSA/AML: Bank Secrecy Act/ Anti Money Laundering

DNFBF: Designated Non-financial Businesses and Professions

EBA: European Banking Authority

FATF: Financial Action Taskforce

FI: Financial Institution

FIU: Financial Intelligence Unit

FSRB: FATF-Style Regional Body

FTZs: Free Trade Zones

GDP: Gross domestic product

GFI: Global Financial Integrity (United States)

HIS: Homeland Security Investigations (United States)

IFFs: Illicit financial flows

IVTS: Informal value transfer system

IFFs: Illicit Financial Flows

LEA: Law Enforcement Authorities

ML: Money Laundering

MVTS: Money Value Transfer Service

NRA: National Risk Assessment

OCG: Organized Criminal Group

PPP: Public Private Partnership

PML: Professional Money Launderers

SAFE: Safe Administration of Foreign Exchange

SBML: Services-based Money Laundering

STR: Suspicious Transaction Reports

TBML: Trade-based Money Laundering

TBML/TF: Trade-based Money Laundering and Terrorist Financing

TBTF: Trade-based Terrorist Financing
TF: Terrorist Financing
TTU: Trade Transparency Unit
UNCTAD: United Nations Conference on Trade and Development
UN ECLAC: United Nations Economic Commission for Latin America and the Caribbean

Chapter One

INTRODUCTION

CHAPTER SYNOPSIS

$

This book begins with the introductory chapter, which presents the background to the study, problem statement, objectives, methodology, contribution of the research to knowledge and practice, and delimitations of the study.

Background to the study

The term "money laundering" describes a range of practices used to disguise the source of illicit profits and integrate them into the legitimate economy. Simply put, a process through which individuals or entities attempt to disguise the origin of illicitly obtained funds, making them appear to be derived from legal sources. This practice allows perpetrators to integrate "dirty" money into the legitimate financial system, making it challenging for authorities to trace and identify these proceeds (Walker, C., 2018).

Other literature (Levi, M.,2002), defined money laundering as 'washing' dirty money so that it appears clean. Corrupt officials and other perpetrators use money laundering techniques to hide the true sources of their income. This allows them to avoid detection by law enforcement and to spend their profits freely. Money laundering in some form is an essential part of most illicit enterprises, although methods vary widely. Large drug-trafficking organizations and corrupt public officials use complex, multi-jurisdictional layering schemes; small-time criminals use simpler strategies.

Money laundering is the 'hiding or the disguising of the proceeds of any form of illegal activity' (Cassara, 2020, p. 19). Money laundering occurs in three recognizable stages:

> *Placement* – depositing the proceeds of crime within financial institutions.

> *Layering* – obscuring the criminal origin of funds through a string of complex transactions; and

Integration – making the funds appear legitimate through legitimate investments.

According to the Financial Action Task Force (FATF) (FATF, 2006) there are three primary methods of money laundering:

✓ Via financial institutions and non-bank financial institutions. Generally, the 'placement' phase of money laundering involves this method, with criminal proceeds deposited in banks, frequently using 'structuring' techniques to avoid arousing suspicion. Financial institutions are also frequently used in the 'layering' phase (e.g. through 'wiring funds to multiple accounts in multiple jurisdictions'), as well as in the 'integration' phase (e.g. through investing criminal proceeds in the stock market).

✓ Cash smuggling between jurisdictions. This frequently forms part of the placement phase, with cash physically moved to jurisdictions where it can be inserted into financial institutions in jurisdictions where the risk of detection is lower.

✓ TBML and other forms of value transfer (e.g. using traditional banking systems such as hawala) – a form of informal value transfer compliant with Islamic law, which involves a network of brokers and does not require the movement of cash or telegraphic transfer – which is not covered by this report.

Fig. 1: Defining money laundering

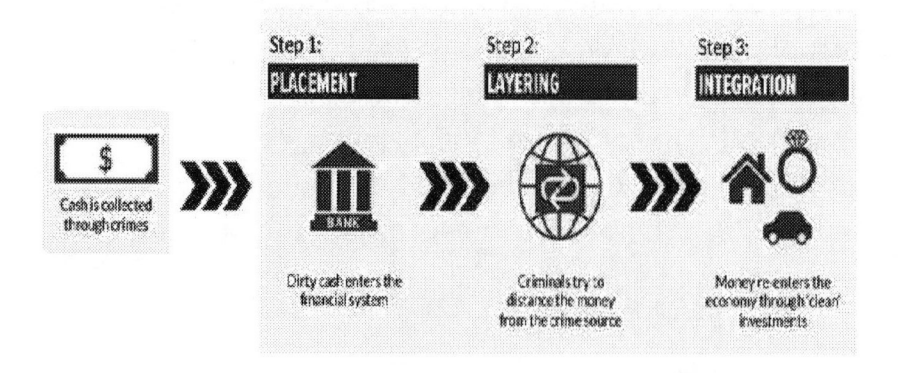

DR NANA KOJO ODI

Using this structure, originally believed to have developed from the West (Levi, M., 1999), (Naylor, R. T., 1999), and (Passas, N., 1999), for the purpose of moving flight capital and tax evading money across borders.

> The aim of trade-based money laundering on the other hand –
>
> Unlike trade-related predicate offences, is not the movement of goods, but rather the movement of money, which the trade transactions facilitate. Just like any other form of money laundering, trade-based money laundering seeks to legitimize the illegal origin of the proceeds of crime.

In the 1960s and 1970s drug dealers stepped into these same channels to move their illicit money across borders (Naylor, R. T., 1999). In the 1980s and 1990s, seeing how easy it was for the drug dealers to do it, other kinds of racketeers stepped into these same structures to move their illicit money across borders. In the 1990s and in the early years of this new century, terrorist financiers also stepped into these same channels to move their illicit money.

The IMF and the World Bank, for example, have estimated that some 2-4 percent of the world's GDP stems from illicit sources. (Agarwal and Agarwal, 2004 & 2006), using regression analysis and forecasts, suggest an even higher level of 5-6 per cent. At this rate somewhere between $2.0-2.5 trillion should flow through the money laundering market on an annual basis. Walker (1999, 2004, 2007) however, claims that this is too low a figure and, using input-output and gravity models, proposes that the true amount is more like $3 trillion per annum. Each estimate is subject to some criticism (cf. Reuter 2007) and are variously said to be overblown—either by media hype, or measurement errors—by as much as +/-20 per cent (Schneider,2008). Despite all this, the consensus remains that the market for money laundering is a significant one.

According to the United Nations Conference on Trade and Development (UNCTAD), Africa loses US$88.6 billion annually to IFFs (Illicit Financial Flows). In the case of Latin America and the Caribbean, the United Nations Economic Commission for Latin America, and the Caribbean (UNECLAC) estimates that from 2004-2013, illicit financial outflows represented 1.8% of regional gross domestic product (GDP) and 3.1% of regional trade, with losses totaling US$765 billion for the 10-year period. Ultimately, IFFs undermine institutions, contribute to insecurity, harm communities and the environment, and deprive countries of much-needed tax revenues.

One of the most prevalent channels for IFFs is through the international trade system. As of 2021, GFI (Global Financial Integrity, United States) estimates that the annual value of trade related IFFs in and out of developing countries amounted to, on average, about 20 percent of the value of their total trade with advanced economies.

Fig. 2: Overview: Trade-Base Money Laundering

Trade-Based Money Laundering: Open-Account Transactions

Trade-based money laundering is the process of disguising proceeds of crime by moving value through trade transactions to legitimize their illicit origin, often by under- or over-invoicing the payment for the goods. In open-account transactions, the buyer and seller negotiate the terms of the transaction, and their banks process the payments for the transaction often without access to the documents underlying the transaction, such as an invoice or a description of the goods.

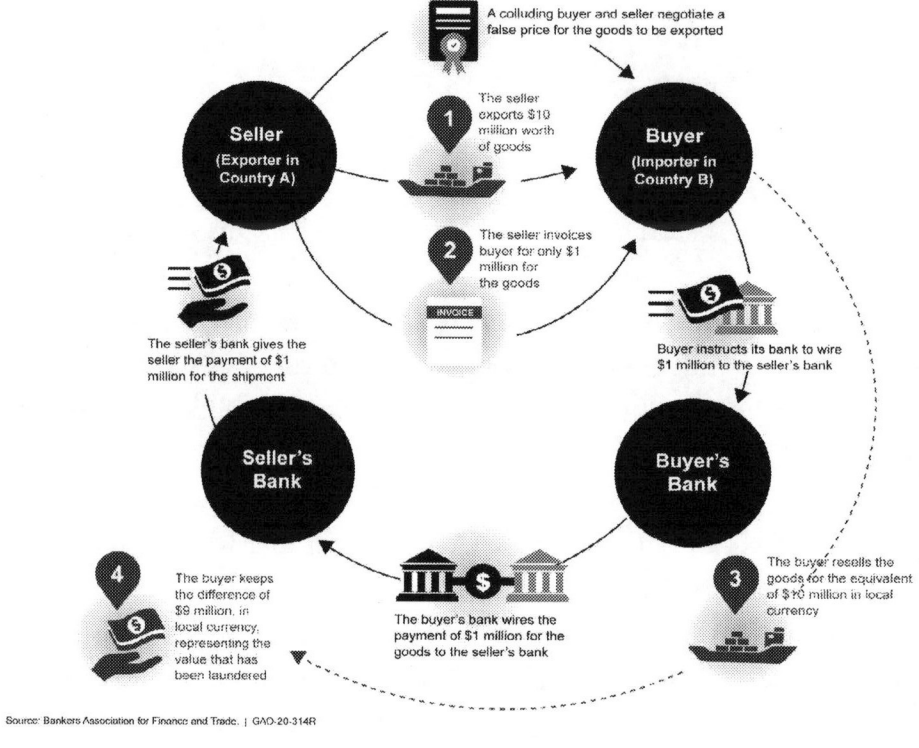

Source: Bankers Association for Finance and Trade. | GAO-20-314R

Problem statement

TBML—as earlier defined, is not the movement of goods, but rather the movement of money, which the trade transactions facilitate. TBML involves acts designed to conceal or disguise the true origin of criminally derived proceeds so that the unlawful proceeds appear to have been derived from legitimate origins or constitute legitimate assets. It is a highly effective way of integrating large volumes of criminal proceeds with legitimate income which is attractive to organized crime groups (OCGs) because it is very hard to detect, track and investigate due to its transnational nature and the complexity of the international trade system.

The global value of money laundering is frequently quoted as being in the order of 2–5% of global gross domestic product (GDP), which would imply a figure between

US$800bn and US$2tn annually. This 'consensus estimate' gained popularity following a 1998 speech by the IMF director general (Camdessus, 1998) and later studies have provided similar estimates (e.g. UNODC, 2011). While this figure appears plausible, it is important to acknowledge that the evidence underpinning it is inevitably highly limited, making it little more than a reasonable best guess. Moreover, this figure may not include TBML (Cassara, 2020)

There is a fine line between TBML and other money laundering methods and in practice, they often overlap. TBML may also result in evasion of income tax and excise and involve other financial crimes, although tax evasion may not be the primary objective. For clarity of analysis and to assist in the understanding of TBML and its ramifications, TBML is defined and differentiated from other types of money laundering and associated activities such as tax evasion.

Bearing in mind the essential features of TBML, TBML is defined here (and developed within the report) as *the use of trade to move value with the intent of obscuring the true origin of funds*. TBML does not include transportation of cash and bearer negotiable instruments, nor does it include the services provided by alternative remittance dealers.

> The dynamics of international trade, involving numerous parties, countless transactions, and interwoven supply chains, provides a fertile ground for money launderers to disguise the origin and movement of their funds. This presents a critical issue for financial institutions, regulatory bodies, and law enforcement agencies, requiring a comprehensive understanding of TBML patterns, vulnerabilities in trade finance, and effective countermeasures to safeguard the integrity of the financial system and prevent criminal organizations from exploiting trade mechanisms for illicit financial activities.

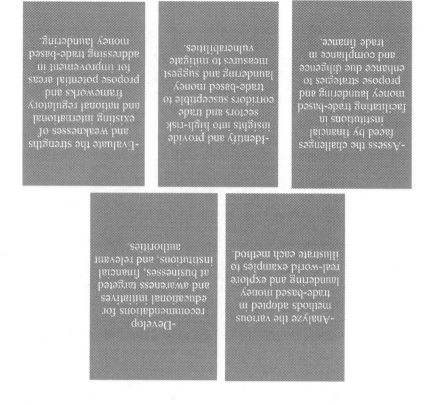

Objectives of the Study

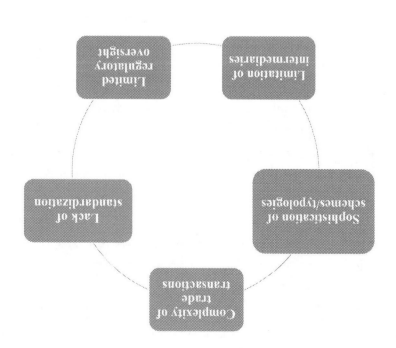

Methodology

Research adopted in writing this book made use of secondary data comprised of a review of publicly available official reports and literature on TBML from a range of international sources. This review of the publicly available literature was guided by consultations with experts and stakeholders and overseas law enforcement, prosecution and regulatory agencies who were identified as having operational information and experience of direct relevance to TBML and its impact on a global scale.

While the latest publicly available information has been used, there are time delays, especially in the release of official statistics, which make it difficult to present completely contemporary information. At present, the information about TBML and its impact is relatively limited. Unlike money laundering using the financial system, TBML is an emerging concept that has had little attention from academic scholars and regulatory and policy bodies.

This review serves as the foundation for identifying gaps in knowledge, theoretical frameworks, and key concepts that guide the subsequent phases of research in TBML. The approach provides a well-rounded understanding of the subject matter and enhances the validity and reliability of the findings, ultimately contributing valuable knowledge to the existing literature and fostering a nuanced understanding of the complexities surrounding TBML.

Significance of the Study

Trade-based money laundering (TBML) is a complex and dynamic challenge that requires ongoing research and practical solutions to enhance our understanding and counter measures against this illicit financial activity. This book makes significant contributions to both knowledge and practice in the field of TBML which is essential for developing effective strategies to detect, prevent, and combat this form of money laundering.

FATF has identified three primary methods of money laundering: the laundering of money through the financial system, the physical movement of money (such as through cash couriers), and TBML.

Contributions to knowledge

The research contributes to a deeper understanding of the various methodologies employed by perpetrators in TBML. This includes over/under-invoicing, multiple invoicing, false descriptions, and phantom shipments. By dissecting these methods, scholars can provide insights into the evolving tactics used to exploit the international trade system.

Furthermore, this book sheds light on gaps and weaknesses in existing legislative and regulatory frameworks. Identifying these gaps allows policymakers to refine and strengthen regulations to keep pace with the evolving nature of TBML.

Contributions to knowledge are exhibited in identifying high-risk trade corridors, sectors, and jurisdictions vulnerable to TBML. Researchers can analyze historical cases and patterns to develop risk assessment models that help authorities prioritize their efforts and allocate resources more effectively.

Contribution to Practice

This book seeks to encourage the establishment and improvement of Trade Transparency Units in various countries as a practical step. Sharing success stories and best practices related to TTUs can guide nations in implementing effective units for monitoring and combating TBML.

Additionally, one of the significant highlights is the need for stakeholders to ensure practical solutions include capacity-building initiatives for law enforcement agencies, financial institutions, and customs authorities. It goes without mentioning that capacity programs can equip professionals with the knowledge and skills needed to effectively detect and develop futuristic anti-money laundering tactics to combat TBML.

Beyond the need for policy amendments, the book establishes and suggests public-private partnerships (PPP) as crucial in practice. Conferences, workshops, and collaborative initiatives bring together government entities, financial institutions, and businesses to share information, expertise, and best practices in combating TBML.

Delimitations of the study

Data Availability

Lack of transparent and comprehensive data on international trade transactions, especially those involving small or medium-sized enterprises (SMEs), can impede a thorough analysis of trade-based money laundering. The author was transparent about data limitations and used available datasets judiciously.

Regulatory Variability

Differences in legislative frameworks and regulatory practices across countries created challenges in standardizing the study. What is considered money laundering in one jurisdiction might not be defined similarly in another. The Author clearly articulated the scope and focus of the study within the context of specific jurisdictions. Compared and contrasted legislative frameworks, and discussed how variations impacted the interpretation and identification of trade-based money laundering.

Dynamics in Trade Transactions

The intricate nature of international trade transactions, involving multiple parties, currencies, and financial instruments, made it challenging to isolate and identify instances of money laundering accurately. The Author recognized the complexity of trade transactions and used a multidisciplinary approach. Combining quantitative analysis with qualitative methods to gain a more comprehensive understanding of the various factors influencing trade-based money laundering.

Chapter Two

TRADE-BASED MONEY LAUNDERING TRENDS

CHAPTER SUMMARY

───────── $ ─────────

This chapter addresses major events arising from the latest TBML activities and how responsible institutions have duly approached these concerns. As an introduction to the latest trends in Trade- Based Money Laundering (TBML), key factors contributing to the movement of illicit financial flows in relation to developed and less developed countries (weaker versus stronger currency location preference). The chapter will also highlight the dynamics involved in the latest trends in Trade-Based Money Laundering.

In the past, there has been a growing recognition of the threat that illicit financial flows (IFFs) pose to the integrity and stability of the global financial system. But in recent past,, with the onslaught of the Covid-19 crisis, concerns are growing that the scale and scope of IFFs could be increasing as authorities are distracted and overwhelmed by the unprecedented economic fallout. Such concerns are especially worse in developing countries, many of which are already characterized by poor governance, weak regulatory oversight, and corruption.

The most recent annual report from Global Financial Integrity (GFI, 2023) on the challenges posed regarding TBML – the illicit movement of money across borders by hiding it within the regular commercial trading system – analyzes the scope and characteristics of global trade-based money laundering and its impact on development, found discrepancies of hundreds of millions of dollars between what nations were officially reporting about the value of their imports and exports with each other over the last ten years. This finding strongly indicates massive levels of IFFs are going undetected through the global trading system.

Fig. 3: Crime typology in money laundering

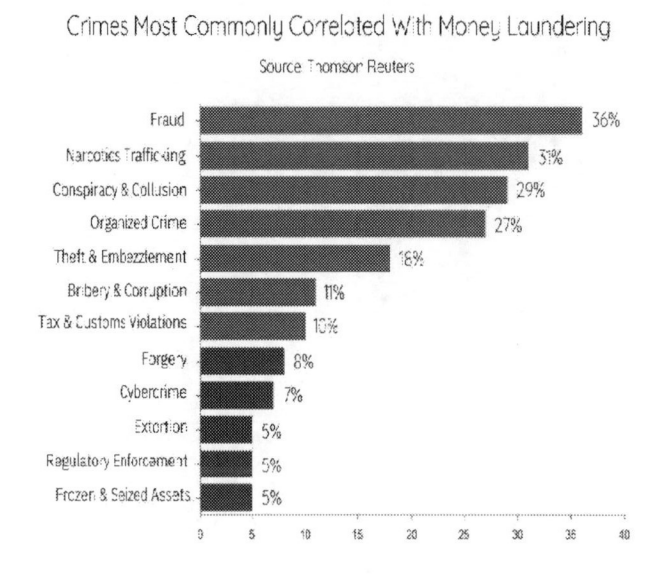

Crimes Most Commonly Correlated With Money Laundering

Source: Thomson Reuters

Fraud	36%
Narcotics Trafficking	31%
Conspiracy & Collusion	29%
Organized Crime	27%
Theft & Embezzlement	18%
Bribery & Corruption	11%
Tax & Customs Violations	10%
Forgery	8%
Cybercrime	7%
Extortion	5%
Regulatory Enforcement	5%
Frozen & Seized Assets	5%

Three major developing events created a new focus of TBML:

Focus 1 - Trade Transparency Units (TTUs)

The U.S. State Department and Treasury Department supported the Immigration and Customs Enforcement Bureau (ICE) of Homeland Security with necessary funding to establish TTUs with Brazil, Argentina, and Paraguay, to analyze both sides of international trade transactions data provided through these partnerships with other countries. One of these investigations was called 'Operation Deluge' and revealed $200 million in Brazilian import duty fraud caused by marking imports at undervalued prices. This investigation resulted in the parties being convicted of income tax evasion in the U.S. This money laundering scheme, detected through Operation Deluge, was said to be the largest in the history of the country as indicated by Brazilian government officials (https://home.treasury.gov).

Focus 2 - The Financial Action Task Force (FATF)

In 2006 the FATF released the report entitled Trade-Based Money Laundering, in which it identified the three major methods used by criminal organizations and terrorist financers to move money for the purpose of disguising its origins and integrating it into the formal economy. Of the three methods, the physical movement of goods through the trade system and the focus of this paper was the most compelling.

Focus 3 - The Federal Financial Institutions Examination Council (FFIEC)

The FFIEC released its first Bank Secrecy Act/ Anti-Money Laundering (BSA/AML) Examination Manual in 2005, which includes key points such as the assessment of a bank's system of managing risk associated with trade financing activities, and the management's ability to implement rules/regulations, monitor the organization and report discrepancies.

TBML represents an important channel of criminal activity and given the growth of world trade, an increasingly important money laundering and terrorist financing vulnerability. In January 1992, Money Laundering Alert published an article on www. moneylaundering.com, which used the average country price versus the average world price for every product to detect TBML via abnormal international trade prices. The initial objective of the research methods used by Zdanowicz was to estimate the amount of money moving out of the U.S due to over-invoiced imports and under-invoiced exports. In addition, all U.S. export and import trade databases from January 1, 1993, to December 31, 1993, in which each commodity/type of good had a 10-digit harmonized code number were gathered.

This method was done to create, maintain and re-check a database, which had all large dollar amount of international trade transactions for the entire year.

This methodology had five features:

✓ Recognizes each country has different trade characteristics.
✓ Analyzes each countries trading history (imports, exports, prices etc.) with the U.S.
✓ Analyzes prices that are 50 percent above or below the average price, determines the amount of over-invoiced imports and under-invoiced exports and the total amount of money that moved out due to these types of invoices.
✓ The same procedure repeated for subsequent years, therefore provides data for three years (93, 94, 95). This methodology was used to set an example for other researchers etc. so that they inculcate a habit of creating yearly trade databases for their convenience.
✓ Shows the amount of money that moved out of U.S. due to abnormal trade prices in: 1993 - \$97.35 B, 1994 - \$116.18 B, 1995 - \$136.76 B.

International trade has some of the most complicated regulations of any sector. International trade is governed by a range of overlapping bilateral agreements, multilateral agreements (between three or more nations) and prevailing international standards from bodies such as the World Trade Organization (WTO), World Customs Organization (WCO) International Civil Aviation Organization (ICAO), International Chamber of Commerce (ICC). And increasingly over the years, we have observed a sharp increase in the implication of unilateral or multilateral trade embargoes, sanctions, and export-import controls on dual use of goods, military items, protected wildlife, selected chemicals, and precursors.

Furthermore, in recent years the Financial Action Task Force (FATF), Bankers Association for Finance and Trade (BAFT), The Wolfsberg Group, the Bank of International Settlements (BIS) and an increasing number of national regulators have contributed to raising trade finance compliance standards.

The WTO, which currently has over 160 members representing almost 99% of international trade, with major decisions being made by the membership, negotiations can be extremely difficult and complex. Sometimes the length of negotiation prevents agreements from materializing. As a result, international trade regulation has somewhat limited, patchy, and complicated controls, leaving the sector exposed to a few loopholes that perpetrators are too willing to exploit.

Additionally, the value of global trade is immense, with millions of high-value transactions being carried out each day. The US Customs and Border Protection recorded that on a typical day in 2019, around 79,000 containers and $7.3 billion worth of goods entered the US through various ports. This volume of traded goods offers an opportunity for criminals to 'hide in plain sight' given that large transfers can easily blend in with legitimate trades. These issues are exacerbated by the paper-based nature of the international trade sector which makes it difficult to apply automation or other innovative solutions. As a result, organizations are often forced to take documentation at face value due to their limited ability to validate its authenticity.

Transnational crime is big business, research places its worth as much as $2.2 trillion each year. These perpetrators need to disguise their illicit profits to benefit from the proceeds within the legitimate financial system.

Key Factors Driving Illicit Financial Flows (IFFs)

One of the key push factors driving illicit financial flows is the economic importance to move wealth from weak to hard currencies in advanced economies (US dollars, British pounds, EU euros, Japanese yen, etc.). Weak currencies are generally subject to higher degrees of volatility on global exchange markets and higher rates of inflation, both of which tend to erode their value over time, whereas hard currencies tend to store the value of wealth more effectively over time.

Additionally, control over assets, wealth, and property rights in developing countries are relatively more vulnerable to politically motivated confiscations and political upheavals as compared to the greater degrees of security and stability in advanced economies.

Tax evasion is another major impetus driving companies and wealthy individuals to engage in trade mis-invoicing to illicitly move value out of developing countries.

On the other hand with pull factors, a major attraction is the greater ability of rich countries and "secrecy jurisdictions," such as tax havens and offshore centers, to store wealth, secure assets and hide illicit finances, drives many to move their wealth out of developing countries.

Latest trends and developments – The dynamics

In the wake of the economic fallout from the Covid-19 crisis, all the dynamics are intensifying, driving up the essence to illicitly move wealth out of developing countries as they are set to crash hard. The global economic slowdown is hitting developing countries across Africa, Asia and Latin America especially hard. Oil exporters have also been hit as global market prices and export revenues have collapsed, and countries dependent upon tourism have similarly seen their incomes suddenly fall. Additionally, for the developing countries that have become increasingly reliant on the remittances of their foreign workers, the World Bank has projected that global remittance flows to low and middle income countries fell by more than $US100 billion in 2021, as a result of the Covid-19 crisis.

A World Bank report (2022) indicates that developing countries will experience serious economic crisis as their exports dry up, and foreign investment capital flees, as their companies and governments are unable to raise new funds in current market conditions. In such circumstances, it will be nearly impossible for them to roll over their foreign currency-denominated debt in international capital markets, which could easily lead to large-scale sovereign debt defaults and the value of their currencies crashing. What's worse is that, while laid off workers in the advanced economies can often benefit from some type of unemployment insurance, most suddenly unemployed workers in developing countries cannot, due to high levels of informality in employment. Consequently, tens of millions are facing sudden economic and food insecurity. The United Nation's World Food Program warned the number of people facing acute food insecurity could double in 2020 from the year before to 265 million and that "the pandemic and lockdown measures combined with rising unemployment and limited access to food could lead to violence and conflict."

For all these reasons, those with wealth are very likely to try to get it out now more than ever, and by whatever means possible. When it comes to concerns about trade mis-invoicing, Europe's top banking regulator, the European Banking Authority (EBA), has singled out the likelihood of international trade as a potential risk. Whereas global trade is presently expected to be slowing down across the board, institutions should scrutinize the legitimacy of those cases in which the value of trade flows have increased, "particularly among customers or regions badly affected by the virus."

In both cases, the common factor is that often regulatory officials lack good data on the actual prices of goods being imported or exported. It is difficult for customs officials looking at declared values on invoices, or bank officials approving trade financing to know if the prices for goods being declared by an importer or exporter are close to actual prices on world markets. For example, Anton Moiseienko of the UK-based Royal United Services Institute, explained, "If a client asks a bank to wire money as payment for goods, it's very difficult for the bank to say whether that payment is adequate, too much or too little." Moiseienko continued, "Because it won't necessarily know what the goods are, what the quality is, and it can be difficult to price them anyway. Conclusively, banks just don't have enough information to be able to say, 'this is trade-based money laundering.'"

Furthermore, for those ports around the world that have remained open and active, there is a secondary risk of possible heightened attempts to bribe officials monitoring the movement of goods. As many countries have closed airports, handling facilities and ports have made it difficult to get goods shipped.

The European Banking Authority (EBA) has noted from past crises, even when overall levels of legitimate financial activity declines, "in many cases illicit finance will continue to flow." In fact, the Financial Crime Enforcement Network (FinCEN), a bureau of the US Department of the Treasury, the UK's National Crime Agency and Europol have already documented an increase in cybercrime, insider trading, fraud and trading of counterfeit goods directly linked to those exploiting the chaos of the Covid-19 crisis.

As advanced and developing countries alike attempt to mobilize large fiscal stimulus packages to keep their economies afloat, this has meant huge bursts of government spending quickly being moved from national to local levels. The emergency nature of such spending often means that regulatory oversight is weakened as corners are cut. The problem is magnified by the world's disrupted supply chains, as those engaged in procurement are under pressure to resort to less well-vetted suppliers. The World Customs Organization (WCO) has warned of an uptick in Covid-19-related fraudulent activities, particularly the trafficking of counterfeit medical supplies, such as face masks and medical gloves.

Additionally, social distancing associated with the economic lockdowns also meant that a great deal of in-person vetting of suppliers and hard copies of supply contracts have been shifted online, with many adopting electronic signatures, digitized documents, and online payment portals for the first time, often before adequate.

Grand corruption, another type of IFFs, is also likely to worsen during and after the crisis. The corrupt officials and those who bribe them utilize existing mechanisms and networks used to hide and launder the proceeds of corruption, channels that are likely to help even in an emergency context, when resources and attention are focused elsewhere and normal standards for supervision, reporting deadlines and due diligence requirements have been loosened. Many such exploits have already come to light, from Saudi Arabia to Uganda to Colombia, for alleged misappropriation of emergency Covid-19 funds.

The Financial Action Task Force's (FATF) response to Covid-19 emphasized the importance of risk-based supervision to ensure authorities use their resources wisely. The group has begun to step up its coordination across its members and regional bodies and observers such as the United Nations (UN), IMF, World Bank, the Organization for Economic Cooperation and Development (OECD), the Egmont Group and Europol on Covid-19 related money-laundering risks. It is using this global FATF network to identify challenges, good practices and policy responses to new threats and vulnerabilities arising from the Covid-19 crisis, and to identify ways to increase information sharing between public sector agencies and banks by leveraging communications with larger institutions and different jurisdictional authorities on new threat information.

Such international support for addressing the problem of IFFs is particularly important now, at a time of major global crisis, when the threat of IFFs takes on an even larger magnitude. But much more assistance and support are needed at the national level in many developing countries. For example, GFI has called for improved interagency collaboration at the national level, as in many developing countries, there is a need for better interagency coordination between financial intelligence units, customs agencies, law enforcement and anti-corruption commissions in identifying and stopping IFFs.

Similarly, developed countries need to lend a helping hand to their developing counterparts in ensuring the integrity of aid and other disbursements during the Covid-19 response period. As Jodi Vittori of Transparency International's Defense and Security Program noted, "Developed nations such as the United States, the United Kingdom and European Union states, as well as multilateral institutions such as the International Monetary Fund, need to make transparency, accountability and anticorruption priority matters in the disbursement of relief funds to developing countries."

As with much of the Covid-19 crisis, what the world does now will have ramifications for years to come.

Chapter Three

TRADE-BASED MONEY LAUNDERING TYPOLOGIES

CHAPTER SUMMARY

———————— $ ————————

The chapter showcases the key Trade-Based Money Laundering typologies which indicate the diverse methods used by perpetrators to exploit trade transactions for money laundering purposes. Hopefully, stakeholders such as authorities and financial institutions would be vigilant in detecting and preventing these tactics to combat Trade-Based Money Laundering effectively.

A. Invoice Fraud

Invoice fraud occurs when someone purposely invoices for more than the correct amount, causing companies to overpay or even pay someone who never offered them goods or services in the first place. In today's interconnected, fast-paced business landscape, countless operations have been simplified and sped up, thanks to the integration of digital tools and platforms. While these advancements have ushered in an era of increased efficiency and globalization, they have concurrently opened pandora's box of vulnerabilities, key among them being invoice fraud. The surge of this form of fraud stands as a stark reminder that with every digital leap, there comes an array of challenges that businesses must grapple with.

Invoice fraud, once a relatively unheard-of concept, has rapidly metamorphosed into a prevalent concern for both large corporations and small enterprises alike. A cursory look at recent statistics paints a daunting picture, the instances of invoice fraud have seen an unprecedented rise over the past decade. This isn't just a number game; these statistics are emblematic of lost revenue, tainted reputations, and in some dire cases, the complete collapse of businesses.

The digitization of business operations, while a boon in many regards, has inadvertently created fertile ground for fraudsters to exploit. The convenience of electronic invoices, swift online transactions, and automated payment systems, while essential for modern businesses, have become the very tools that crafty cybercriminals manipulate to their advantage. They exploit the vast digital terrain, which is often inadequately guarded, to siphon off funds, disrupt operations, and sow seeds of distrust.

However, this is not merely a narrative of gloom. It's a wake-up call. As we delve deeper into the intricacies of invoice fraud, its manifestations, and repercussions, it is crucial to approach the topic with a dual perspective: understanding the threat while simultaneously recognizing that the solutions, with the use of innovative technology, vigilance, and a proactive mindset.

Mispricing

Mispricing, otherwise known as under-invoicing or over-invoicing, is a common method used in TBML whereby goods are deliberately declared at an incorrect value. Mispricing in trade-based money laundering (TBML) is a technique that involves falsifying the value, volume, or type of goods or services in an international transaction to move money illicitly across borders. Trade mis-invoicing is the largest component of illicit financial outflows measured by Global Financial Integrity.

By fraudulently manipulating the price, quantity, or quality of a good or service on an invoice submitted to customs, perpetrators can easily and quickly shift substantial sums of money across international borders.

Over-invoicing looks at inflating the value of goods or services on invoices to overstate the cost of the goods being traded. The excess amount is then transferred to the criminal organization.

Under-invoicing, on the other hand, involves declaring a lower value for goods or services on invoices, allowing the sender to retain the extra funds. This technique can also be used to evade taxes and customs duties.

As a result, firms can transfer millions of dollars between one another while shipping goods that are worth next to nothing. This can often involve misrepresentation of quality to influence the pricing on the invoice.

Examples:

- *A company exports cement bags worth $2,000,000 but invoices the importer for $20,000,000. The importer sells the cement bags for the fair market value of $2,000,000 and transfers $18,000,000 of criminal proceeds to the exporter.*

- *A company exports computers worth $20 million in total but invoices the importer for $500,000. The importer sells the computers for the fair market value of $ 20 million, gaining $19,500,000. This allows* *the exporter to transfer $19,500,000 of criminal proceeds to the importer.*

Broadly, there are four primary reasons to mis-invoice trade:

Money laundering: Criminals or kleptocrats may seek to launder the proceeds from crime or corruption.

Directly evading taxes and customs duties: By under-reporting the value of goods, importers are able to immediately evade substantial customs duties or other taxes. Additionally, under-reporting the value of exports also allows companies to understate their revenues, and in turn, reduce their income tax liability.

Claiming tax incentives: Many countries offer generous tax incentives to domestic exporters selling their goods and services abroad. Criminals may seek to abuse these tax incentives by over-reporting their exports.

Avoiding capital controls: Many developing countries have restrictions on the amount of capital that a person or business can bring in or out of their economies. Individuals or entities attempting to break these capital controls often mis-invoice trade transactions as an illegal alternative to getting money in or out of the country.

The simple act of making and sending an invoice does not result in a legally binding agreement. If that were the case, anyone could send someone else an invoice and demand payment. On the contrary, an invoice is only a legal document once both sides agree to the content within.

As the Chinese government recently announced moves to crackdown on illicit capital inflows through trade mis-invoicing, Global Financial Integrity (GFI) finds that US$400 billion flowed illicitly into China from Hong Kong via trade mis-invoicing between 2006 and the first quarter of 2013. The estimates by Global Financial Integrity were released in an article by GFI Junior Economist Brian LeBlanc on the website of the Thomson Reuters Foundation.

The Chinese government has expressed concern that illicit inflows aimed at circumventing capital controls are fueling currency and housing speculation in the country. Mr. LeBlanc—utilizing official trade data from the IMF and the Hong Kong Customs and Excise Department—finds that US$101 billion was illicitly smuggled into China via export over-invoicing in 2012, with an additional US$54 billion flowing in illegally in just the first quarter of 2013. Total illicit inflows via trade mis-invoicing dating back to 2006 are pegged at a massive US$400 billion. GFI believes these are the first public estimates of the amount of illicit money flowing into China from Hong Kong.

One measurable way which Chinese regulators alluded to is a process known as "export over-invoicing". This involves the deliberate falsification of export invoices to make it seem as if exporters are sending more goods out than they are. By doing this, an exporter can smuggle in additional capital—under the guise of legitimate trade payments—before diverting the foreign capital (illegally) into other more lucrative investments like bonds or real estate.

Although no estimates from **S**uspicious Activity Filing Environment (SAFE), a system that allows financial institutions to report suspicious activities to FinCEN, were provided, over-reported exports are easily detectable through a comparison of bilateral trade statistics. As earlier indicated, a comparison of China's trade with Hong Kong shows that an alarming $101 billion of exports simply disappeared at the Hong Kong border in 2012 alone, with an additional $54 billion smuggled in during the first quarter of 2013. The cumulative amount of foreign exchange brought illicitly into China masked as trade payments from Hong Kong since the first quarter of 2006 adds up to an astounding $400 billion.

Putting this into perspective, the $101 billion of foreign exchange brought in through illicit exports represents about 40 percent of the $253 billion of legal net FDI that China received from abroad during the same year. Such large sums of money have the potential to be destabilizing and are most likely being used to fuel further currency and housing speculation within the country.

Coupled with that, there also appears to be a direct correlation between the amount of hot money entering China through export over-invoicing and the US Treasury bond rate. As rates have declined in the US due to the Fed's monetary stimulus that began in 2009, export over-invoicing has increased in lockstep.

A similar event happened in the 1997 crisis, when Alan Greenspan began increasing the federal funds rate following a rebound from the early-1990s recession in the United States. This combined with a strengthening US dollar contributed to investment fleeing Asian markets for greener pastures in a recovering US economy.

As many countries attempt to process customs transactions quickly, to promote trade and boost economic growth, trade mis-invoicing has become a fairly low-risk endeavor for criminals—especially those who only moderately mis-invoice their transactions by, say, five to ten percent.

Multiple-Invoicing

Multiple-Invoicing involves issuing duplicated invoices for the same shipment of goods, therefore inflating the value transfers through the finance system. Multiple-Invoicing can also be used in fraud schemes where inflated credit is generated and received for the collateral goods. Creating multiple invoices for the same shipment, often with varying amounts, to confuse authorities and facilitate the movement of additional funds.

> **Example:**
>
> *A company exports an order for hospital equipment worth $10,000,000, but issues 5 duplicate invoices to the importer. Companies may process the invoices through multiple banks to avoid detection. This allows the importer to transfer the value of the duplicate invoices ($4,000,000, plus the original $10,000,000) to the exporter, while using trade documents that reflect accurate prices and quantities.*

The human element

As businesses fortify their digital defenses against the multitude of cyber threats, a subtle but potent vulnerability often remains overlooked: the human element. Behind the abstract concept of "invoice fraud" lies a very tangible and complex interplay of human behaviors, decisions, and emotions. While technology has enabled and amplified the reach and sophistication of fraud, it is human actions and oversights that often facilitate its success.

The unintentional catalyst

Lack of training: Not every employee is versed in the latest fraud detection techniques or understands the intricate methods fraudsters employ. Without proper training, even glaring red flags can go unnoticed.

Overwhelm & oversight: Employees in large corporations can be swamped with numerous tasks daily, making it easy to miss inconsistencies in an invoice, especially if it mirrors legitimate ones.

Miscommunication: A breakdown in communication between departments or team members can lead to duplicate payments or approvals of suspicious invoices without proper verification.

The conscious error

Collusion with external parties: Some invoice fraud cases arise from an internal employee conspiring with an external fraudster. Such employees may provide sensitive information or deliberately approve fraudulent invoices.

Phantom suppliers: A rogue employee might create fictitious vendors and generate fake invoices to funnel money directly into their pockets.

Manipulation of real invoices: An employee with access to financial data might intercept and alter genuine invoices, changing bank details or inflating the amount to siphon off funds.

The fraudster's art

Social engineering: Beyond mere data and numbers, seasoned fraudsters exploit human psychology. They might impersonate trusted vendors, invoke urgency, or use authority figures to bypass rational scrutiny.

Preying on trust: Long-standing vendor relationships, built over years, can be exploited. An unexpected change in an invoice from a trusted vendor might be overlooked, based on the presumption of trust.

Exploiting fear: Fraudsters can create a sense of panic, such as threats of service discontinuation, to pressure quick and thoughtless payments.

B. Shipment Fraud

Today's worldwide shipping is carried out by individuals and organizations hailing from a vast variety of countries and locations. The current global economy is the product of a time of relatively unrestrained trading when compared to earlier worldwide economies, which were mostly driven by imperial power. In contrast, the previous global economies were largely driven by imperial power. Shippers, charterers, shipowners, bankers, insurers, importers, and exporters are all members of the modern maritime community.

The system that was constructed for the transfer of products is straightforward and effective, and the sea continues to serve as the lifeblood of international trade. Since the delivery of goods typically takes some time, it is the practice in international business for the buyer to pay the seller before the customer receives the products being purchased. The letters of credit system, in which banks serve as intermediaries, has proven to be effective, and the paperwork involved in these transactions is more important than the products themselves (Jennings et al., 2006). As a direct consequence of this, an international marine contract will often involve many parties. Fraud is a particularly devious form of criminal activity that occurs when one party to a maritime contract wrongfully acquires money or items that belong to another party associated in the carrying and funding of the transaction.

The risk posed by fraud is that it could destabilize the system by putting users' faith in jeopardy. Forgers, swindlers, and cheaters are drawn to the convenience of the system that governs international trade, which makes it susceptible to their activities. When one of the various parties involved in an international business transaction intentionally misleads another about some truth or occurrence in connection with marine activities to dishonestly collect money or products, this is an instance of maritime fraud. A significant effort on the part of numerous parties is required to pull off such frauds (Jones, 2011).

There is evidence of fraudulent activity in the business sector that dates all the way back to the time of the Roman Empire. According to the description provided by the International Maritime Bureau, "a transaction involving international trade involves several actors," including a buyer, a seller, a shipowner, a charterer, the ship's expert or crew, insurance, a lender, a broker, or an agent. It is referred to as maritime fraud when one of these parties acquires money or products from another party to whom, on the surface, he has assumed defined trade, transport, and financial duties. The growth in instances of fraud in the marine industry can be attributed to several variables, including the following: As a result of the growing pressure placed on shipowners to acquire new customers, many of them have neglected to undertake sufficient due diligence when communicating with possible new business partners.

Additionally, criminals are increasingly turning to new methods, such as hacking computers. Because con artists are always one step ahead, it is essential to stay one step ahead of them as well, particularly as more and more transactions are carried out electronically. A better level of security, of course, comes at a "cost," not only in the form of investments in new and enhanced technology and processes, but also in terms of the potential impact on economic prospects. To achieve the right level of skill and competence in one's business, in addition to having an awareness of the many schemes and con jobs that are available, is necessary. Because there are so many different people and locations involved in even the most fundamental A >>B journey, the shipping industry is rife with opportunities for con artists to take advantage of those who aren't well-versed in the complexities of international trade. For example, there are so many different people and places involved in even the most basic A >> B excursion. Because the parties are in different countries, it may be difficult or even impossible to perform "physical checks" between them. This is because the parties are required to conduct business at "arm's length" or through intermediaries such as brokers and banks.

In recent decades, maritime fraud has developed into a sector that is both highly profitable and relatively minimal risk. In the late 1970s, maritime criminal activity reached an all-time high, and the upward trend has only continued since that time. The obvious implication of this is that it begs the question of what kinds of schemes could be at work during a maritime con. It is general knowledge that a single international commercial transaction involves many distinct types of enterprises, including vendors, purchasers, shippers, charterers, captains, crew, port authorities, inland hooligans, banks, and insurance companies.

The crime of maritime fraud is perpetrated when one of these individuals takes advantage of another to steal money or products. As a direct result of this, the term "marine fraud" refers to a particular type of fraud that takes place in the maritime industry. Documentary fraud, which occurs when a document or signature is faked, as well as chartering frauds, as well as the intentional or false loss or destruction of cargo, barratry, the scuttling of ships, and other similar schemes, are all examples of this (Jennings et al., 2006).

The target of a fraudulent scheme involving marine transactions could be located anywhere in the world. The con artist is completely indifferent to the victim's ethnicity, religion, or ideology. There are a variety of different sorts of fraud that can occur in the maritime industry, and there is enough evidence to suggest that organized criminal gangs are responsible for a sizeable portion of these cons as well as other related offences. For a respectable number of years, the shipping sector has been working fruitfully based on verbal agreements that are contained within a system. The ongoing infiltration of organized groups into the maritime industry is the one factor that raises the greatest level of worry regarding the fight against marine crime and fraud. In the 1920s, scuttling and other forms of intentional ship damage achieved some attention (Jones, 2011).

Other forms of intentional ship damage included: it was not until the 1970s that it was rediscovered as a pioneering new art form; prior to that, it had fallen into obscurity. For example, after her cargo was taken, the infamous Salem had to be cast off into the ocean (Jones, 2011). The days of owners purposefully sinking old and worthless ships have been replaced with schemes that are conducted by a ring of con artists that is more sophisticated, financially stable, and strategically planned (Jennings et al.,2006). There are many different guises that marine cargo fraud can take, ranging all the way to the deliberate destruction of over insured commodities. It is possible to commit fraud by overestimating the value of the ship as well as the goods it carries (Jones, 2011).

Over or under-shipment

Over or under-shipment is an instance where a seller either ships more goods than previously agreed with the importer, thereby transferring greater value to the importer, or the exporter ships fewer goods than agreed, transferring greater value to the exporter.

Over-shipping or short shipping works through a difference in the invoiced quantity of goods and the quantity of goods that are shipped.

The buyer or seller gains excess value based on the payment made. Variations can also involve the quality of the goods declared which can likewise create value discrepancies.

> *Example:*
>
> *A company exports tons of bacon, but falsely reports it as weighing 0.5 tons on transaction documents and therefore worth less. The importer pays for 0.5 tons and then resells the full ton, which transfers value to the importer.*

Phantom Shipments

Some Organized Crime Groups OCGs go a step further and invoice shipments of goods that don't take place or do not exist. This technique considers generation of invoices for goods or services that do not exist, creating fictitious transactions to move money across borders. Due to the paper-based nature of the sector, OCGs can produce fraudulent documents and make it appear as though goods have been shipped, and if the process seems legitimate, money is exchanged. This is also referred to as ghost shipping.

> *Example:*
>
> *- A shoe manufacturing exporter invoices its import partner for a shipment of male wears. The invoice reflects a reasonable price and quantity, but the shipment container was empty (i.e. the goods were never shipped). The importer nevertheless pays for the goods, transferring value to the exporter.*

This is an interesting concept, where the buyers and sellers collude with each other and orchestrate a scheme where fake invoices and other shipping documents travel alone with no merchandise associated with it.

The seller sends the invoices to the buyer for the goods which are not dispatched and in some cases the goods don't even exist. The buyer who receives no goods makes the payments for the goods which were never received. The TBML takes place when these two parties viz. the buyer and the sellers are in two different countries through using phantom shipments. This typical TBML scheme involves collusion on both sides of the import-export transaction and the transfer of value across borders. Financial institutions need to have a sound compliance program. There are many red flags associated with such transactions. Financial Crime Compliance teams of the banks need to identify them.

Growth of the e-commerce transactions is very helpful in the financial crimes associated with the phantom shipments. Sellers can register their products on these marketplaces such as Amazon or Alibaba. It requires very little or in some local marketplaces no Know Your Customer (KYC) documents. Sellers can sell the commodities at inflated prices and the buyers would purchase them at agreed prices with the sellers. The eCommerce company can be an unsuspecting participant in the Trade Based Money Laundering scheme and can dispatch the scrap for millions of dollars and take an omission in the same.

In certain cases of the phantom shipments, where the delivery will never be dispatched, the nature of amazon transaction would be changed from Fulfilled by Amazon to Self-fulfillment and the goods would never get into the ship to be delivered, however the payments would be routed through the marketplaces and the seller receives clean money from the remittance of Amazon.

TBML under this concept is especially risky because it is closely tied to a host of other types of violations, such as violations of U.S. export control and sanctions laws, as well as the U.S. Foreign Corrupt Practices Act.

C. Shell and Front Companies

A shell company is a business entity that has no real operations or assets. It is often used for money laundering by hiding the source and destination of illicit funds.

Front companies on the other hand are entities that serve as a front or cover for illicit activities, often used to facilitate money laundering, fraud, or other illicit financial transactions. They are designed to create a semblance of legitimacy while hiding the true purpose and ownership behind them. Front companies are considered to be fully functioning companies with the characteristics of a legitimate business, serving to disguise and obscure illicit financial activity. Businesses that deal with high volumes of cash are typically used as a front for criminal activities and money laundering.

However, Shell and Front companies are part of a broader subject. that goes beyond of the scope of this write-up. They are basically used to reduce the transparency of ownership in the transaction.

Examples:

- *A shell company purchases jewelleries with funds derived from criminal activities and then sells the goods to buyers in high-risk countries with minimum due diligence. The proceeds are then directed back to the shell company*

- A front company may over-invoice or under-invoice the goods it exports or imports and receive or pay the difference in cash from or to a third party.

Shell entities play an integral role in global money laundering operations. These shell organizations, found throughout the world, offer money launderers secrecy to build networks in various jurisdictions to layer their cleansing operations (Teichmann 2017; Crumbley et al., 2019). Reducing liability for its participants remains a focus of these entities, and common legal structures include asset protection trusts, limited partnerships (LPs), limited liability companies (LLCs), and company foundations (Baradaran et al., 2014; Willebois et al., 2011). In 2011, a World Bank study found that perpetrators in 70 percent of large-scale corruption cases relied on the secrecy of shell entities to hide the identity of the beneficial owners (Global Witness 2013).

Shell companies serve broad interests but usually possess no significant assets while facilitating the global movement of large sums of money. Their physical presence typically represents no more than a mailing address that may be shared by many other shell companies, have no employees, and produce little or no economic value (FinCEN 2006; Anonymous 2013; Hubbs 2014). One building in Delaware represented the domicile for 285,000 firms, which was ten times higher than all registered companies in the Isle of Man, a noted offshore bank secrecy haven.

The Paradise Papers, comprising 13.4 million documents, originated mostly from the Bermuda-based firms Appleby and Asiaciti Trust (Murphy 2017). The released information provided details on how money launderers and others conceal their ownership of major assets, protect their funds from governmental taxing authorities, and secretly conduct their business. Most activities the Paradise Papers exposed were technically legal, yet the public response across many countries was highly negative with many actions deemed unethical (Murphy 2017). The need for concealment attracts money launderers to jurisdictions with tight financial secrecy laws and practices.

In 2009, the Tax Justice Network (TJN) launched an online database that demonstrates how legal, judicial, and regulatory structures within jurisdictions contribute to the environment of financial secrecy (Christensen 2012). From this database, the TJN generates its Financial Secrecy Index, a global ranking based upon financial secrecy and the scale of offshore financial activities. The TJN estimates that secrecy jurisdictions use concealment and anti-disclosure laws to attract $21 to $32 trillion dollars of private financial wealth (TJN 2018).

The Financial Security Index (FSI) highlights inaccuracies found within traditional stereotypes of financial secrecy. Many of the world's leading financial nations such as the U.S., Switzerland, Hong Kong, Singapore, and the UK offer the greatest financial secrecy, not small, palm-fringed islands (TJN 2018; Browning et al., 2018). Observers note that some of the world's most dangerous criminals establish shell entities in the U.S. because its system of shell entities and secrecy restrictions promote an environment conducive to money laundering and other crimes (Szubin 2016).

Different business structures emerged over time to promote commerce in different environments. Yet persons with either honorable or illicit objectives may establish domestic and offshore entities such as LLCs, asset protection trusts, Limited Liability Partnerships (LLPs), International Business Companies (IBCs), and private interest foundations (PIFs). Parties may use these entities to hold title to illegally obtained assets, launder money, open and fund financial accounts in the names of their entities, and cloak beneficial ownership from authorities. Criminals often use shell entities to commit their crimes, with money laundering being especially popular.

A single instance of shell companies facilitating money laundering occurred in 2014 when Hewlett-Packard A.O. (HP Russia) agreed to pay more than $100 million in fines for violations of the Foreign Corrupt Practices Act (FCPA)18 (Athanas 2010; Deming 2006). The plea agreement details how executives within HP Russia created a multimillion-dollar slush fund they used to bribe Russian government officials (U.S. Department of the Justice (DOJ) 2014). HP Russia laundered the payments through an intricate web of shell companies and bank accounts. This example reveals how such abuses are compounded because many jurisdictions permit shell entities to own and manage other shell entities (FinCEN 2006).

Recently, the U.S. Justice Department accused 33 persons of using a web of more than 250 shell entities to launder over $2.5 billion through the international banking system to help North Korea fund its weapons program and bypass international sanctions (Benner 2020). These multiple layers of cloaked ownership make it extremely difficult for forensic accountants and law enforcement officials to identify the beneficial owners.

Background to Shell and Front Entities

Limited Liability Companies (LLCs)

Various parties misuse LLCs because they can be owned and managed anonymously in many jurisdictions, though the level of ownership transparency differs by jurisdiction (Government Accountability Office (GAO) 2006). LLCs provide members with the same limited liability afforded to corporate shareholders while usually providing pass-through taxation benefits. LLCs serve common tasks when used as shell entities, such as owning other entities, holding bank accounts, or serving as a transfer point of funds.

Different ownership structures of LLC shell entities exist, but a popular method uses bearer shares, where ownership resides with whomever holds the certificate (Biedermann

2015). Though not valid in the U.S., this form of LLC is commonly used in many jurisdictions while its lack of ownership transparency facilitates illegal activities and prevents the disclosure of beneficial owners. Organizers can easily form LLC shells and build layers across multiple jurisdictions to create a confusing path for forensic accountants, auditors, and investigators (Martinez 2017).

The U.S. remains popular world-wide among those seeking to avoid ownership transparency. Some jurisdictions, such as Wyoming and Nevada, offer no regard for LLC ownership transparency and make the disclosure of beneficial ownership virtually impossible (Vail 2017). Given this environment, authorities observe that more money laundering occurs with U.S. LLC shells than those of any other country (Sharman 2013). A prime example of LLC shell abuse occurred in U.S. v. Rosbottom et al., when the courts convicted Harold Rosbottom and Ashley Kisla of multiple charges with Rosbottom's bankruptcy, including conspiracy to commit money laundering. Rosbottom was a wealthy entrepreneur who owned over a hundred businesses and who employed Kisla, his girlfriend.

Prior to filing for bankruptcy, Rosbottom began withdrawing company funds and held 17 cashier's checks totaling over $1.8 million payable to him personally that were not disclosed on his bankruptcy personal financial statement in June 2009. At that time, Rosbottom asked his attorney to form a Texas LLC with the name N73CL, a reference to a plane Rosbottom wished to acquire. Rosbottom also requested his attorney to form Westwind II, an LLC owned solely by Kisla. In late June, Ohio River LLC, a Rosbottom LLC, received deposits of $545,000, and these funds were wired the next day to an account owned by Houma Inn, another Rosbottom LLC. The funds were used to purchase 50% interest in an airplane, yet the courts determined these transactions proved Rosbottom and Kisla committed money laundering and intended to make it more difficult for the government to trace and identify the nature of the funds.

International Business Companies (IBCs)

An International Business Corporation (IBC) operates as an offshore entity using a traditional corporate structure with articles of incorporation and company directors. An IBC targets non-residents of the jurisdiction in which it is sited, yet it cannot engage in economic activities within its situs jurisdiction. Most offshore jurisdictions apply strict confidentiality regulations upon IBCs, so public registers do not identify their shareholders and directors.

The corporate structure requires IBC shareholders to elect directors, yet the board of directors may run the IBC with little regard to most shareholders. In some areas, the board may make large capital distributions and deplete share capital by ignoring capital retention (Offshore 2005). The lack of restrictions for shareholder distributions makes the

IBC a convenient vehicle for illicit money laundering and the often-legal movement of funds to different jurisdictions.

Corporations and individuals find IBCs useful to shift profit streams from high tax countries into offshore jurisdictions with lower tax rates or tax treaties with other nations. For example, more than 140 businesses in London, New York, and Hong Kong have a unit in the British Virgin Isles, a tax-neutral hub (Houlder 2017). Conversely, money launderers benefit from the ability of IBCs to obscure the money trail for forensic accountants, government officials, and law enforcement.

Limited Liability Partnerships (LLPs)

LLPs represent excellent places to hide assets, for in a typical scheme, the general partner provides assets to trusted associates, friends, or family members to invest in the partnership (TJN 2018). These investors become limited partners with no personal legal liability for the debts of the business, nor can they take an active role in operating the business. A different scenario portrays the general partner providing funds to an LLP of which he is the sole limited partner and then transferring the partnership interest to a trust of which he is the sole trustee and beneficiary.

Trusts

Trusts represent another tool abused by money launderers since they provide a separation of legal and beneficial ownership (Danforth 2002). Within trusts, a settler grants legal control of assets to a trustee. A settler who establishes the trust can increase protection for the trustee by including a spendthrift provision. Self-settled spendthrift trusts, also known as asset protection trusts, create a framework where the settler also receives the benefits from the trust. These specialized trusts represent a thriving, multi-billion-dollar business for banks, trust companies, and estate planners in the U.S. and abroad (Morse 2008). The popularity of asset protection trusts stems from their ability to provide beneficiaries with greater privacy and autonomy than traditional business entities.

Trusts also benefit from their historical exclusion from central registries that list names of relevant parties (Fidelity Investor 2017). Yet when the identities of beneficiaries must be disclosed, trusts can generate opacity to the ownership structure by declaring the beneficiary to be an LP, LLC, or another trust (Simser 2008).20 Those who want to commit money laundering or other financial crimes often use offshore asset protection trusts (OAPTs) in four ways:

✓ Integrate illicitly obtained funds into an economy as "clean assets" (i.e., money laundering) (Silets and Drew 2001);

- ✓ Move legitimately obtained funds into an economy to be used for illegal purposes (i.e., reverse money laundering) (Arce 2009);
- ✓ Hide legitimate assets from creditors with bona fide claims or from spouses in divorce proceedings (Silets and Drew 2001); and
- ✓ Hide legitimate assets for purposes of tax evasion (Silets and Drew 2001).

The users of OAPTs want to launder assets through enough layers of the trusts to obscure the presence or source of funds from anyone, including forensic accountants and law enforcement (Zagaris 1999). By achieving this goal, parties can control their assets without being named as a beneficiary or trustee, where estimates suggest that OAPTs safeguard $1 to $5 trillion in assets (Maxwell 2014). Those seeking to misuse OAPTs for illegitimate purposes often rely upon layering and misdirection, which obscures the identity of the wrongdoer and creates the misimpression that the wrongdoer does not control the OAPT.

The federal case, U.S. v. Brennan, when the Second Circuit upheld Robert Brennan's conviction for bankruptcy, provides examples of the misuse of OAPT features. Brennan owned and operated First Jersey Securities, Inc. (FJS), a brokerage trading in penny stocks. Brennan and FJS were found guilty of securities fraud in 1995 and ordered to pay $75 million to 500,000 customers. Near the end of his trial for securities fraud, Brennan created an OAPT known as the Cardinal Trust and funded it with $4 million in bearer bonds.

Shortly after the securities fraud trial, FJS and Brennan filed for bankruptcy, but Brennan did not disclose Cardinal Trust's assets in the bankruptcy action and grew its assets to $22 million by mid-1997. Brennan laundered $12 million in trust assets to acquire a gambling boat that conducted legitimate business; he also moved the Cardinal Trust's venue twice to avoid detection. The court convicted Brennan of money laundering and other offenses and sentenced him to over nine years in prison.

Shelf Corporations

Shelf corporations reflect companies formed to have no activities until purchased by those wanting to conduct legitimate or illicit business quickly. The new owners often buy domestic and offshore shelf companies since they avoid the burdensome legal filing requirements while gaining immediate ownership without shares having been offered (Weiss 2011). Some shelf entities also possess established bank accounts that transfer to the new owners. Once acquired, the new owner may benefit from the established credit and tax history of the shelf company, which further enhances its credibility (Willebois et al., 2011). Authorities observe that the lack of accurate, recorded information about shelf entities can create almost insurmountable obstacles to identifying beneficial owners by auditors, forensic accountants, and law enforcement officials.

Private Interest Foundations

Private interest foundations (PIFs) act as alternatives to trusts by offering a structure for asset protection and estate planning in civil law jurisdictions, though some common law areas have begun adopting them (Berbey de Rojas 2008). The first PIF was introduced in Liechtenstein in 1926 and has expanded to other jurisdictions known for financial secrecy, such as: Panama; Aruba; the Bahamas; Costa Rica; the Seychelles Islands; and Antigua (Wiggin 2008).

The operators of PIFs, as with asset protection trusts, often use them to conceal entities, assets, and the identity of individuals. Although no official structure exists for a PIF, jurisdictions around the world specify common features. Panama represents a good example of the emphasis on secrecy; it does not require foundations to keep financial records or submit tax returns, though the country oversees more than 400,000 registered PIFs and offshore corporations (Thompson 2010).

Four common features exist within PIFs:

- ✔ Founder—the person or entity, analogous to a trustee, that forms the foundation in the public registry.

- ✔ Foundation Council—this group serves the same function for a PIF as a board of directors does for a corporation. The public registry lists the names and passport numbers of council member when the foundation is established.

- ✔ Protector—the person or entity that ultimately controls the foundation. Immediately upon establishment, the council appoints a protector through a notarized private protectorate document. The protector remains anonymous because the document is private and not publicly registered.

- ✔ Beneficiaries—a PIF does not have owners but rather beneficiaries. The protector appoints the beneficiaries through either a private letter or a formal set of bylaws which remain confidential (Boschini 2006; Berbey de Rojas 2008; Elements 2017; Aspen Group Limited 2012).

PIFs provide a significant amount of secrecy and flexibility, thus money launderers and others engaged in illicit activities find them useful vehicles. Secrecy abounds since no legal requirements exist to disclose the identities of a PIF's founder, beneficiary, or protector, and no requirement exists for the filing of tax returns or financial statements. The foundation charter may be signed by an attorney without disclosing the name of the founder, and a

PIF may engage in any business or civil transaction in any part of the world and in any currency. Thus, PIFs prove useful for those wishing secrecy for their operations.

Nominees or Nominee Directors

Recruiting a nominee as company director represents another effective method to conceal the identities of beneficial owners of a shell company. The nominee holds bare legal title for another yet may act in place of the other in a limited way and may receive and distribute funds for others (Martinez 2017). A nominee can be a person who either has close or no links to the true beneficial owner; examples of nominees are provided in U.S. v. Monaco. In this dispute, Jimmy Monaco, a Florida-based drug trafficker and pirate, selected various family members to serve as nominees while he was in prison.

These nominees, including his parents, committed acts such as: burying money in back yards; hiding funds in safe deposit boxes in their names; and engaging in transactions on various real properties throughout Florida. Many shell entities throughout the world use the same nominee directors since some of these directors actively market their services globally. Authorities observe that only 28 nominee directors either control or have established more than 21,000 companies, with a large portion of these individuals having some involvement with criminals or their organizations (Ball 2012).

In this environment, organizers can also register shell entities anonymously to further disguise their ownership and operate without scrutiny from authorities, including major jurisdictions like Switzerland; the U.S.; Hong Kong; Singapore; Germany; Taiwan; China; Japan; and Canada (Ball 2012; TJN 2018). In 2014, the International Consortium of Investigative Journalists (ICIJ), representing journalists from 65 countries, pooled their information and published the incorporation records of shell companies and directors (some nominees). The publication revealed how many shell companies formed a global network that was highly intertwined with their nominee directors (http://tinyurl.com/jwxbg2z). Thus, money launderers find great opportunities within this network of shell companies that provides such high levels of secrecy.

Researchers identify three primary reasons that allow money launderers to conceal their identities as beneficial owners and operators of entities. One reason reflects the legal framework in many jurisdictions that reduces ownership transparency. Secondly, those who abuse shell entities can conceal their identities by hiring the services of gatekeepers such as accountants, and lawyers. Finally, the layering of multiple shell entities across jurisdictions makes it virtually impossible for forensic accountants and law enforcement authorities to identify the beneficial owners.

This environment provides money launderers global access to shell entities while generating effective barriers to uncovering the identities of beneficial owners. Governments and international organizations claim to recognize the value of ownership transparency and the exchange of information about entities. Yet organizations such as the FATF, OECD, G8, and G20, have only recently begun to cooperate on collecting and exchanging information about beneficial ownership and money launderers.

Proponents of greater coordination advocate for the creation of ownership registries, yet jurisdictions also confront the complications about registries such as infringing on privacy, placing excessive burdens on financial institutions, undermining national sovereignty, preventing bank secrecy, and violating contractual relationships. Overall, progress exists in global efforts to improve information exchange and ownership transparency of shell entities to prevent money laundering, though the pace of change appears fitful and modest.

D. Round-Tripping

Round-tripping is a methodology often associated with trade-based money laundering (TBML) involving the movement of funds out of a country, often through international trade transactions, and then brought back into the same country, creating the illusion of legitimate economic activity. This process involves a cyclical flow of funds, with the primary objective of disguising the illicit origin of money.

Foreign Direct Investment (FDI) also promotes the use of more advanced technologies by domestic firms through capital accumulation in the domestic country. Mauritius has very huge investment opportunities (seafood and exploitation of deep-sea water for oil). However, in terms of FDI, the DTAA between India and Mauritius has been and still remains the most beneficial of all treaties that India has had, and that Mauritius has been able to obtain a niche in terms of FDI in India, being the largest source for nearly 10 years.

Since 2000, 35.18 billion USD have been routed through Mauritius making Mauritius the main contributor of FDI to India. Today, India is the No.1 recipient of funds through its diaspora. Most of these bilateral investments are routed through Mauritius. Despite the Euro-zone crisis, Mauritius has an economic growth of nearly 4% which is a clear representation of the growth potential the country has.16 It helps to increase domestic markets competition, create job opportunities, and enhance business and economic growth.

As global production and corporate structures of MNEs have evolved over the years, their investments have become a sophisticated set of financial transactions that are hard to monitor and classify by the home and host countries. Mauritius ranks 32nd among 175 countries and second in Africa, after South Africa, and eases for doing business (World Bank's "007 Doing Business Survey, 2007) after various economic reforms, business facilitation, investment opportunities and incentives.

By transferring knowledge, FDI will increase the existing stock of knowledge in the host country through labor training, transfer of skills, and the transfer of new managerial and organizational practices. FDI will also promote the use of more advanced technologies by domestic firms through capital accumulation in the domestic country. Some researchers on elasticity and capital (Lucas, 1993) found that the FDI inflows are more elastic with respect to cost of capital than wages and more elastic with respect to aggregate demand in exports than domestic demand. Indeed, determinants of FDI inflows to transition economies like some countries in the central Europe for example are country risk, labor cost, host markets size and gravity factors during the period 1994-1998.

Major determinants of FDI flows are market size, openness of the economy, infrastructure, macroeconomic stability such as inflation, wages, human capital, natural resources just to name a few but it was also demonstrated that some determinants such as infrastructure and inflation are both positively related while the wage rate is negatively associated to FDI flows. These determinants are also important factors influencing the FDI flows in South Asian countries principally.

Several authors found that there is a positive and significant relationship between market size and FDI flows though FDI seems to be more determined by wealth effects rather than market size effects and may even be insignificant on FDI flow. There are also conflicting views concerning labor cost and FDI. Some authors affirmed that the FDI and labor cost are closely associated whereas other authors declared that labor cost and FDI are negatively related since a higher labor-cost would result in a higher cost of production and in turn reduced FDI inflows. Whether trade openness is a positive and significant determinant of FDI has also been studied and has been found to have a positive impact on FDI.

Similarly, the development of higher educational institutions could turn Mauritius into a 'knowledge hub' of the Indian Ocean attracting high-value-added foreign investment by increasing the visibility of the country regionally (such as student fairs on the African country) and internationally, provided there are infrastructures facilities such as electricity, water, transportation, telecommunications as they contribute positively to FDI. Some studies have been carried out and it has been found that market size and growth are important determinants of FDI.

In some cases, MNEs (Multinational Entities) invest in a country through intermediaries in third countries, constituting the so-called indirect forms of FDI. These investments can be undertaken through permanently established foreign affiliates or through established SPEs in a third country. While this form of investment should be considered FDI, the nationality of the immediate investor and the ultimate beneficiary owner will not match. In the case of the SPE, the immediate investor is in fact only a financial entity. MNEs might prefer to invest in a country indirectly through another country perhaps to take advantage of better tax regimes or less stringent corporate governance—through corporate inversions—, or simply to leverage the cultural and geographic proximity—through nearshoring. For example, when the German telecom company, Deutsche Telekom, wanted to invest in the former Yugoslav Republic of Macedonia, it did so through its majority owned affiliate Magyar Telekom (Hungary) in order to benefit from the proximity between these two countries. Nevertheless, the investment in Makedonski Telekom was as if it came directly from Germany, with all the top management being German rather than Hungarian."

Nonetheless, in some cases, the specific intent might be to conceal the identity of the ultimate investor for various reasons. Furthermore, indirect FDI flows may also capture funds that are not necessarily foreign sourced. These are domestic funds channeled through offshore centers to the local economy in the form of direct investment. As discussed later in detail, such behavior by domestic investors is called round tripping and is triggered by various reasons including special treatment of foreign investors, tax benefits, as well as governance and institutional concerns.

Furthermore, the essential motivation might be to circumvent the institutional and financial shortcomings of their country of origin rather than just tax avoidance or illegal activities. Firms in developing countries might choose to operate from locations that offer them more services and opportunities to access financing through listing companies in more developed stock exchanges or raising funds in international markets. For example, Hong Kong, with its better-developed international stock and financial markets, offers opportunities for Chinese firms to raise funds in the stock market or solicit better lending terms.

Consequential to this case, the round-tripped investment may not translate into a loss for the host country, China. This might be an important step for developing country firms to expand their operations globally. For example, in the case of South African Breweries (SAB), the company was originally established in South Africa but later moved its main listing on the London Stock Exchange in 1999 to raise capital for acquisitions. The company made several global acquisitions, changed its name to SABMiller plc, and became a globally successful firm.

The firm now operates in South Africa through its local subsidiary, and its assets are now classified as foreign direct investment. Similarly, companies might use round tripping to escape from the perceived excesses in state control/intervention ("system escape" motive) and other uncertainties in the country of origin. Similarly, operating from more "stable" locations, where the regulatory environment is perceived as being more advantageous, constitutes the so-called "safety nests" motive. For example, Mittal Steel (now part of ArcelorMittal), whose founders were born in India but resided in London, registered their firm in the Netherlands to circumvent the heavy and bureaucratic Indian regulations, and they have expanded their operations both in India and globally.

Mittal Steel acquired the European steel company Arcelor in 2006, and the merged company, ArcelorMittal, chose Luxembourg for its official headquarters and is now the world's largest steel producer. Investing through another country might enable firms to secure some of the protections extended by the bilateral investment treaty (BIT) of the transit country. For example, treaty rights such as property rights and protections related to investor-state dispute settlement (ISDS) options are especially important to firms that undertake capital-intensive and risky projects. This is because the ISDS option provides an explicit option to foreign investors to bring their claims to domestic courts or international arbitration under the framework of UNCITRAL or ICSID.

This allows the round-trip investor to choose the forum where a dispute with the host country will be settled, while a domestic investor would automatically be subjected to the national court system without the option of international arbitration. The circular movement of funds through these trade transactions creates the illusion of legitimate economic activity. However, the actual goods or services being traded may be of little or no value, and the primary purpose is to launder the funds.

Example:

- *"Entity A" initiates the process by sending funds out of the country. This can be done through various means, such as over-invoicing, under-invoicing, or other trade manipulation techniques. To cloud the illicit transaction, "Entity A" may set up front companies or use existing ones to conduct these trades.*

- *In other cases, "Entity A" may create fictitious transactions, inflating the value of goods or services on invoices, or even fabricating entirely false trade transactions. This is done to give the appearance of a legitimate economic exchange. Once the funds have been moved out of the country, they are brought back into the same country through another set of international trade transactions. This can involve a different set of front companies or intermediaries.*

Chapter Four

RISK AND MITIGATING FACTORS TO TRADE-BASED MONEY LAUNDERING

CHAPTER SUMMARY

—— $ ——

Trade-based money laundering (TBML) can occur in various sectors, but certain industries are at higher risk due to factors such as the complexity of their supply chains, high transaction volumes, and the potential for manipulation of trade documentation. Inclusively, the chapter assesses mitigation factors to financial institutions serving as a pivot to the Trade-Based Money Laundering ecosystem.

High Risk Sectors to Trade-Based Money Laundering

Identifying vulnerable business sectors is crucial in proactively addressing the risks associated with trade-based money laundering and trade-based terrorist financing. The types of businesses at risk of trade-based money laundering (TBML) exploitation are varied, and various small and medium-sized companies are previously identified in different TBML schemes.

The risk indicators provided are derived from a sampling of the data received by the FATF and the Egmont Group of FIUs during the Trade-Based Money Laundering (TBML) project. The risk indicators are designed to enhance the ability of public and private entities to identify suspicious activity associated with this form of money laundering. By no means is this a conclusive list. While several indicators identified may not appear to have a direct or exclusive connection with TBML and may be indicative of other forms of money laundering or another illicit activity, they may nonetheless be relevant when trying to identify TBML.

The investigations involved large multinational companies as well, where through the overseas branches or subsidiaries trading relationships were developed in distributing goods into the newer markets.

A risk indicator demonstrates or suggests the likelihood of the occurrence of unusual or suspicious activity. The existence of a single indicator in relation to a customer or transaction may not alone warrant suspicion of TBML, nor will the indicator necessarily provide a clear indication of such activity, but it could prompt further monitoring and examination, as appropriate. Similarly, the occurrence of several indicators could also warrant closer examination. Whether one or more of the indicators suggests TBML is also dependent on the business lines, products or services that an institution offers; how it interacts with its customers; and on the institution's human and technological resources.

These sectors are not inherently involved in illicit activities, but the nature of their operations and the global movement of goods and funds make them susceptible to abuse by money launderers. Regulatory authorities, financial institutions, and businesses in these sectors must implement robust anti-money laundering (AML) measures and conduct thorough due diligence to mitigate the risks associated with TBML.

The corporate structure of a trade entity appears unusually complex and illogical, such as the involvement of shell companies or companies registered in high-risk jurisdictions.

Trend Scenarios:

- A trade entity lacks an online presence, or the online presence suggests business activity inconsistent with the stated line of business, e.g. the website of a trade entity contains mainly boilerplate material taken from other websites or the website indicates a lack of knowledge regarding the product or industry in which the entity is trading.
- A trade entity displays a notable lack of typical business activities, e.g. it lacks regular payroll transactions in line with the number of stated employees, transactions relating to operating costs, tax remittances.
- Owners or senior managers of a trade entity appear to be nominees acting to conceal the actual beneficial owners, e.g. they lack experience in business management or lack knowledge of transaction details, or they manage multiple companies.
- A trade entity is registered or has offices in a jurisdiction with weak AML/CFT compliance.
- A trade entity is registered at an address that is likely to be a mass registration address, e.g. high-density residential buildings, post-box addresses, commercial buildings, or industrial complexes, especially when there is no reference to a specific unit.
- The business activity of a trade entity does not appear to be appropriate for the stated address, e.g. a trade entity appears to use residential properties, without having a commercial or industrial space, with no reasonable explanation.
- A trade entity, or its owners or senior managers, appears in negative news, e.g. past money laundering schemes, fraud, tax evasion, other criminal activities, or ongoing or past investigations or convictions.

- A trade entity maintains a minimal number of working staff, inconsistent with its volume of traded commodities.
- The name of a trade entity appears to be a copy of the name of a well-known corporation or is very similar to it, potentially to appear as part of the corporation, even though it is not actually connected to it.
- Contracts, invoices, or other trade documents display fees or prices that do not seem to be in line with commercial considerations, are inconsistent with market value, or significantly fluctuate from previous comparable transactions.
- Contracts, invoices, or other trade documents have vague descriptions of the traded commodities, e.g. the subject of the contract is only described generically or nonspecifically.
- Trade or customs documents supporting the transaction are missing, appear to be counterfeits, include false or misleading information, are a resubmission of previously rejected documents, or are frequently modified or amended.
- Contracts supporting complex or regular trade transactions appear to be unusually simple, e.g. they follow a "sample contract" structure available on the Internet.
- The value of registered imports of an entity displays significant mismatches to the entity's volume of foreign bank transfers for imports. Conversely, the value of registered exports shows a significant mismatch with incoming foreign bank transfers.
- Commodities imported into a country within the framework of temporary importation and inward processing regime are subsequently exported with falsified documents.
- Shipments of commodities are routed through a few jurisdictions without economic or commercial justification.
- A trade entity makes very late changes to payment arrangements for the transaction, e.g. the entity redirects payment to a previously unknown entity at the very last moment, or the entity requests changes to the scheduled payment date or payment amount.
- An account displays an unexpectedly high number or value of transactions that are inconsistent with the stated business activity of the client.
- An account of a trade entity appears to be a "pay-through" or "transit" account with a rapid movement of high-volume transactions and a small end-of-day balance without clear business reasons, including: – An account displays frequent deposits in cash which are subsequently transferred to persons or entities in free trade zones or offshore jurisdictions without a business relationship to the account holder. – Incoming wire transfers to a trade-related account are split and forwarded to

nonrelated multiple accounts that have little or no connection to commercial activity.

- Payment for imported commodities is made by an entity other than the consignee of the commodities with no clear economic reasons, e.g. by a shell or front company not involved in the trade transaction.
- Cash deposits or other transactions of a trade entity are consistently just below relevant reporting thresholds.
- Transaction activity associated with a trade entity increases in volume quickly and significantly, and then goes dormant after a short period of time.
- Payments are sent or received in large round amounts for trade in sectors where this is deemed unusual.
- Payments are routed in a circle – funds are sent out from one country and received back in the same country, after passing through another country or countries.

Free Trade Zones (FTZs) are also emerging as being especially vulnerable to TBML. FATF defines FTZs as 'designated areas within countries that offer a free trade environment with a minimum level of regulation'. FinCEN has identified TBML red flags that are specific to FTZs and FTZs were the subject of a recent money laundering report by FATF (FATF 2010; FinCEN 2010). Although a country like Australia for example, does not have any FTZs, they are of general concern to Australia and Australian interests because FTZs are part of the international trade network.

The number of FTZs has rapidly increased and there are now approximately 3,000 FTZs in 135 countries (FATF 2010). In 2007, total exports from FTZs were estimated at US$400b (FATF 2010). While FTZs have existed throughout the twentieth century, the globalization of the world economy over the last few decades has seen an expansion in the number of FTZs. But FATF (2010: 3) has also observed that the liberalization of trade barriers in the FTZs has made them 'highly attractive for illicit actors who take advantage of this relaxed oversight to launder the proceeds of crime and finance terrorism.'

Mitigations of financial institutions – TBML

Back in 2006, Financial Action Task Force (FATF) emphasized on new measures and strategies for banks to combat money laundering and terrorist funding in its report on TBML. As per the report, FATF highlighted the fact that with new standards applied, other money laundering techniques are becoming more effective. And there's a high possibility that trade based money laundering will grow more attractive. Moreover, very little attention is paid to combat the abuse of the international trade system currently.

Challenges in identifying and countering TBML exist at both the public and private sector levels, with a lack of understanding, awareness, and collaboration both domestically and internationally.

A new publication analyzing the scope and characteristics of global trade-based money laundering (TBML) finds that this illicit activity poses complex problems for law enforcement while also undermining global development. Indeed, while various estimates put TBML activity in the hundreds of billions, or even trillions of dollars annually, "a comprehensive mapping of known TBML [court] cases worldwide from 2011 to 2021" identified just US$60 billion in money laundering, according to the paper. Highlighting the development impact, the study noted that "when TBML goes unchecked, it has adverse effects on economies and societies as it perpetuates criminal activities …corruption, and tax evasion."

The paper, Trade-Based Money Laundering: A Global Challenge, was co-authored by Global Financial Integrity (GFI), Transparency International Kenya and Advocates Coalition for Development and Environment (ACODE) and draws on the technical and regional expertise of each of the organizations – based in the United States, Colombia, Kenya and Uganda, respectively. The study analyzes the numerous challenges of TBML from a global policy perspective.

The publication describes TBML as "disguising the proceeds of crime [by] moving value through the use of (legitimate) trade transactions." The report provides an in-depth analysis of the most common TBML methodologies, which include over- and under-invoicing of goods; misrepresentation of goods being shipped; multiple invoicing of goods; over- and under-shipment or phantom shipments; the black-market peso exchange; and the use of informal value transfer systems. Mis-invoicing was the most common methodology, representing 63 percent of cases.

To date, the focus of anti-TBML initiatives has primarily been on TBML using merchandise, but TBML using the services trade presents a much more significant challenge. Global trade in services provides greater opportunities for money laundering than trade in merchandise because fraud is more difficult to detect and prove. The intangible nature of services makes supply difficult to determine. Unlike merchandise, services are also less likely to be standard, so anomalies in value and price are less apparent and more difficult to substantiate. It is also common and lawful to include retainer and penalty payments which are payable even if the service is not actually supplied. While trade description fraud covers most TBML, it is not used in all TBML schemes. Case Study 4 in the FATF (2006: 12) Typologies Report outlined a detected case of TBML using intangibles. This scheme involved the following steps:

- The personal identification numbers (PINs) of these calling cards are sent to Bangladesh and sold for cash; and

— The cash is given to the Bangladeshi counterpart to settle the US operator's outstanding account.

— An alternative remittance system operator in the United States for example wants to transfer funds to his Bangladeshi counterpart to settle an outstanding account.

— The US operator deposits US dollars into his bank account and then wires the money to the corporate account of a large communications company to purchase telephone calling cards.

— To avoid the scrutiny that would have been attracted by remitting the funds using the financial system.

As the FATF (2006: 12) commentary on the case study explained: In this case, rather than simply wiring the funds to his Bangladeshi counterpart, the US operator chose to minimize the risk of detection using the international trade system. Interestingly, the operator's scheme does not depend on fraudulently reporting the price or quantity of the goods in order to transfer the funds required to settle the outstanding account. In addition, the calling cards are not actually exported.

Trade based money laundering has become a growing concern since the publishing of FATF report. According to the Global Financial Integrity analysis, from 2005-2014, the illicit cash flow to and from emerging and developing countries was 12-24% of their total trade. Not forgetting the potential damage using these funds, is more than a trillion-dollar problem. For years, regulatory authorities and the international trade sector have worked together to address the rising issue. Authorities such as FATF have issued various guidelines to assist banks in combating money laundering.

For decades, anti-money laundering (AML) detection software has been rules-based, creating a problematic two-fold legacy: first, much true criminal activity goes undetected because criminals can learn the rules and then evade them. Second, rules-based AML systems create an inordinate amount of false positive alarms, diverting investigative resources from pursuing genuine Suspicious Activity Reports (SARs). FICO has developed and deployed machine learning and artificial intelligence (ML/AI) systems that address both shortcomings, helping one client, a global bank headquartered in Asia, to achieve a 57% reduction in alert false positives.

Trade based money laundering is often hard to detect because of its nature. One of the biggest challenges that make it difficult for compliance officials to identify TBML is non-documentary trade. In a non-documentary transaction, banks get limited access to information depending upon the transaction structure and the institution's policy. For instance, the bank may only have the name, address, and account number of the seller, and buyer's name and account number.

In such scenarios, the trade occurs without any human intervention like wire transfer.

Banks cannot identify the underlying trade flows for international transactions in a non-documentary trade. Even in a wire transfer, very little information is available that does not suffice for the bank's validation system. Banks only intervene if the transaction instructions are unclear, or a sanction stops the transaction itself for further review.

Banks must understand their customers and their businesses using a comprehensive due-diligence assessment that may include the volume and the type of goods or services. Customer profiles can help banks to validate the flow of transactions and ensure their authenticity.

A recent study conducted by BNY Mellon "Global Payments 2020: Transformation and Convergence" notes a number of evolving trends and challenges. These include:

- ✓ Post-pandemic shift to a new world order with associated changes to the relative importance of different currencies.
- ✓ Trade flows are being reshaped by the increasing engagement of developing markets.
- ✓ A shift away from established documentary trade payment and financing mechanisms toward less complex and less expensive open-account terms.
- ✓ New payment and financing solutions (such as the Bank Payment Obligation or BPO) aimed at supporting global supply chains, along with the expectation of near real-time settlement of financial transactions.
- ✓ New tools and technologies that could address challenges related to TBML—such as the use of fraudulent documentation and the general lack of visibility in trade transactions.
- ✓ Evolution of traditional trade finance models from paper and process-intensive models to a data-driven, automated decisioning mode.

Chapter Five

CONCLUSION AND RECOMMENDATIONS

CONCLUSION AND RECOMMENDATIONS

$

This study on TBML, has reaffirmed the conclusion of earlier studies that TBML is an important channel for criminal organizations and terrorist financiers to move money or value to disguise its illicit origin and to integrate it into the formal economy. The rapid growth in the global economy has made international trade an increasingly attractive avenue to move funds through goods and services. There are instances brought out in this Study where the veil of international trade was deliberately created to launder the proceeds of crime. TBML is a sophisticated and evolving method used by individuals and entities to disguise the illicit origins of funds through international trade transactions. TBML involves intricate schemes that take advantage of the complexity of global trade, including the use of multiple transactions, mispricing, and the creation of fictitious trade documentation. Money launderers continuously innovate to stay ahead of detection efforts.

Certain industries, such as import/export businesses, precious metals and stones, textiles, electronics, and others with complex supply chains and high transaction volumes, are at higher risk for TBML. However, TBML can occur in any sector involved in international trade. Regulating and monitoring international trade poses significant challenges due to the diversity of industries, cross-border transactions, and the sheer volume of goods and services moving globally. Cooperation among regulatory bodies and international collaboration is crucial to combat TBML effectively. Technology plays a dual role in TBML. While it can be used by criminals to facilitate illicit transactions, it also offers opportunities for advanced monitoring and detection through data analytics, artificial intelligence, and machine learning.

Successful prevention and detection of TBML requires collaboration among governments, financial institutions, law enforcement agencies, and businesses. Information sharing and coordination enhance the ability to identify and combat illicit financial activities. Governments globally are working to strengthen regulatory frameworks to address TBML. These efforts include improving due diligence requirements, enhancing transparency in trade transactions, and implementing measures to detect and prevent mispricing and other manipulation techniques.

Businesses involved in international trade must prioritize due diligence to identify and mitigate the risks associated with TBML. This includes robust Know Your Customer (KYC) procedures, monitoring trade transactions for suspicious activities, and staying informed about evolving TBML techniques. The use of advanced technology, combined with ongoing training for financial professionals, customs officials, and law enforcement personnel, is crucial in building a proactive and effective defense against TBML.

International organizations, such as the Financial Action Task Force (FATF), play a key role in setting global standards and guidelines for combating money laundering, including TBML. Countries are encouraged to align with these standards and participate in collaborative efforts.

The international trade system is clearly subject to a wide range of risks and vulnerabilities that can be exploited by criminal organizations and terrorist financiers. In part, these arise from the enormous volume of trade flows, which obscures individual transactions; the complexities associated with the use of multiple foreign exchange transactions and diverse trade financing arrangements; the commingling of legitimate and illicit funds; and the limited resources that most customs agencies have available to detect suspicious trade transactions.

This study provides a number of case studies that illustrate how the international trade system has been exploited by criminal organizations. It also has made use of a detailed questionnaire to gather information on the current practices of more than thirty countries. This information focuses on the ability of various government agencies to identify suspicious activities related to trade transactions, to share this information with domestic and foreign partner agencies, and to act on this information.

While various jurisdictions may have different levels of preparedness for identifying and investigating TBML, the general recognition of its existence and of its future potential underscores its significance. In fact, international trade remains a viable option for movement of value even in those jurisdictions that do not have a well-developed financial or banking sector. Thus, TBML is a concern for the international community even though it may presently impinge upon various jurisdictions without the same impact. Moreover, as the standards applied to other money laundering techniques become increasingly effective, the use of trade-based money laundering can be expected to become increasingly attractive.

Furthermore, efforts should also be made to raise financial institutions' knowledge of TBML and related risks. Financial Intelligence Units (FIUs) can play a critical role in producing sophisticated analysis on TBML schemes – including reporting entities (SAR/ STR data).

Reference to the Sarbanes- Oxley Act on transparency in the United States, financial institutions must report potentially suspicious activity (including trade-related transactions) to FinCEN. Analyzing various trade based money laundering schemes and the red-flag indicators issued by FATF, it all comes down to one major thing, i.e. Know your customer or know your client (KYC) to combat money laundering. An effective AML compliance program makes it obligatory for banks and financial institutions to cross-link the know your client data and regular business alerts.

The report concludes with an analysis of current policy efforts as well as recommendations for ways to bolster the fight against TBML going forward. These recommendations include:

- ✓ Conduct education campaigns and raise awareness of TBML and its risk factors.
- ✓ Convene inter-agency task forces, since combating TBML requires close coordination among numerous government agencies.
- ✓ Implement national beneficial ownership registries to prevent shell and front companies, a common thread in TBML cases worldwide.
- ✓ Ensure that beneficial ownership information extends to trade, especially foreign companies doing business in the country and shipping companies involved in international trade.
- ✓ While efforts have been made to strengthen international information exchange, ensure that this information exchange occurs in real time so that importing and exporting countries can respond more quickly.
- ✓ Utilize new technologies to assess pricing of trade transactions, especially since mis invoicing was one of the most common methods of TBML identified.
- ✓ Ensure that national anti-corruption strategies cover international trade and ports.
- ✓ Strengthen supervision over free trade zones, which may have simplified tax processes but should nonetheless have appropriate, robust measures in place to combat TBML.
- ✓ Since customs agencies are on the frontline in the fight against TBML, ensure that they have the adequate financial, human, and technological resources to do their job effectively.

One of the major obstacles in devising future strategies to tackle TBML has been the lack of reliable statistics relating to it. Most jurisdictions do not distinguish TBML from other forms of Money Laundering (ML). Hence, they have reported that they do not maintain separate statistics for TBML. While the trade data is collected, maintained, and analyzed by customs they neither have a legal mandate to undertake TBML investigations nor do they have training and competence to utilize such data to combat TBML.

As already pointed out in this book any strategy that focuses only on the trade sector leaving out the corresponding elements of the trade finance sector would be inadequate to tackle TBML. Having a warehouse of trade finance data within financial institutions without correlating such data to that of the trade sector will not allow effective targeting of TBML.

It is evident from the feedback from most of the jurisdictions that sharing of the information obtained domestically and internationally has impediments. These impediments relate to inadequate and delayed response, restrictions on the use of the information furnished and insistence on confidentiality or secrecy clause which hamstring its evidential value. More than 50% of the jurisdictions reported having initiated TBML investigations on referrals from other agencies. Again, more than 50% of the jurisdictions reported seeking information from foreign jurisdictions. Laying platforms for effective and prompt sharing of information domestically and internationally can go a long way to combat TBML.

Information relating to the trade finance products remains concentrated within the financial sector. Often the financial institutions are not aware of the significance of the information held by them to TBML investigators. A TBML investigator would need to obtain crucial data from financial institutions and correlate that with the information available in the trade sector to sieve 'TBML-laced' transactions from the predominantly genuine trade flows.

Based on the analysis of patterns, modus operandi, and red flags, four techniques of TBML relating to trade finance have been formulated. The four techniques are: cash inflow payments; third party payments: segmental modes of payment; and alternative remittance payments. These four techniques are those which have been most used by criminal syndicates to support the practice of abusing the trade sector.

Data needed to combat TBML remains dispersed over various domestic sectors. Practices to compile and collate the statistics and data relevant to TBML vary among jurisdictions. There is a need to have common formatting of how TBML statistics are to be recorded and maintained so that trends are more easily identifiable. If centralization of data and statistics is not presently possible then access of competent authorities to such statistics and data should be ensured.

Cross-referencing data relating to trade and trade finance can be the starting point for adopting a risk-based approach. Such an approach will not only lead to prioritization of limited resources but will also facilitate genuine trade without compromising the necessary governance over TBML. A risk-based approach will help capture crucial trade data along with providing an ability to keep track of its corresponding payments data. To ensure efficient real time delivery of analysis the adopting of an electronic platform may be essential. Monitoring foreign exchange may be an option for some jurisdictions in identifying anomalies to detect TBML. one of the findings of the project team is there exists an acute need to correlate trade data with the foreign exchange data of a jurisdiction to detect TBML and identify cases wherein value is moved across countries in the form of goods without corresponding outgo of foreign exchange as its payment.

As an example, the development of a foreign exchange monitoring system to cross-reference trade related data based on an electronic platform. By working out trends and past performances the system conducts some risk analysis to select risk-prone foreign exchange transactions for more specific scrutiny. There is a capacity to systematically target TBML. Capturing data on trade and trade finance in standard format across the jurisdictions will ease cross-referencing for discovering trade anomalies leading to detection of TBML.

Correlating such findings with systematic compilation of foreign exchange data can foster efficient strategies to prevent and combat TBML. Domestic Task Forces. Multiple agencies are associated either directly or indirectly in fighting TBML. One way forward to combine the respective competencies of relevant authorities for combating TBML is to form domestic taskforces. Taskforces focused on TBML investigations will need to have the ability to utilize the expertise of each agency without comprising its functional skills. It is suggested that to be successful the task force must set its modes of communication and interaction.

In this regard an initiative by the World Customs Organization (WCO) to develop the concept of Globally Networked Customs (GNC) for exchange of information may turn out to have significant strategic value. TBML Focused Training. TBML focused training is an absolute necessity for the anti-TBML strategy to succeed. Customs, ML investigating LEA, FIU, Tax Authorities and Regulators have all identified a pressing need for more focused training so that their personnel can have an adequate knowledge base to detect, prevent and combat TBML.

Inter-linkages of tax frauds and customs violations with TBML also need to be explained. The significance of domestic coordination and of international cooperation to tackle TBML must be conveyed during training programs. Further, as many private players are involved in international trade, they need to be apprised of concealed TBML threats in any outreach programs that are conducted. Thus, capacity building among all competent authorities and private industry is an important component of any successful strategy to prevent and combat TBML.

In conclusion, TBML remains a significant challenge in the fight against money laundering. Ongoing efforts to enhance regulatory frameworks, promote international collaboration, leverage technology, and strengthen due diligence practices are essential to mitigating the risks associated with trade-based money laundering.

REFERENCES/BIBLIOGRAPHY

ADB, Asian Development Bank Manual on Countering Money Laundering and Financing of Terrorism, 2003.

ADB, ADB Technical Assistance to Thailand, Three-Year Action Plan, November 2006.

ADB/OECD, Anti-Corruption Initiative for Asia and the Pacific, Curbing Corruption.

Alldridge, P. (2008). Money laundering and globalization. Journal of Law and Society, 35(4), 437–463.

AMLO, A Compendium of Anti-Money Laundering Laws and Regulations.

AMLO, Annual Report 2004.

AMLO, Annual Report 2005.

AMLO, The Asia Europe Meeting (ASEM) Anti-Money Laundering Project – Research.

AMLO, Thailand Jurisdiction Report for July 2005 to July 2006 at APG Annual Meeting.

Anonymous. (2013). The missing $20 million. The Economist, February 16.

Anonymous. (2016a). Tax haven or … tax hell? International Tax Review, May 26, 1–4.

Anonymous. (2016b). Corporate ownership and corruption: How to crack a shell. The Economist, 419, 56.

Annop Likitchitta (Legal Expert), Frequently Asked Questions regarding AML, 1 April,1999.

Anti-Money Laundering Act B.E. 2542 (1999).

APG, The APG Mutual Evaluation Report on Thailand, adopted at APG Annual Meeting, June 2002.

APG and FATF, Jurisdiction Reports at Joint FATF/APG Typologies Meeting.

APG, Typologies http://www.apgml.org/frameworks/

APG, Overlapping Memberships of Multilateral Institutions, September 2007 http://www.apgml.org/jurisdictions/http://www.apgml.org/jurisdictions/docs/36/

APG, Asia Pacific Group on Money Laundering Secretariat.

Arce, B. (2009). Taken to the cleaners: Panama's financial secrecy laws facilitate the laundering of evaded U.S. taxes.

Article: Another nail in the coffin of Thai democracy, by John Ungphakorn, Bangkok Post, 10 October 2007.

ASEAN, 2001 ASEAN Declaration on Joint Action to Counter Terrorism, Bandar Seri Begawan, 5 November 2001.

ASEAN, Work Program to Implement the ASEAN Plan of Action to Combat Transnational Crime. Kuala Lumpur, 17 March 2002.

ASEAN, Transnational Crime and Terrorism http://www.aseansec.org/4964.htm.

ASEM AML Project Consultants, ASEM AML Project Consultants' Technical

Assistance Needs Analysis Report on Thailand, February 2003, 3 December 2003 distributed by UNODC.

ASEM AML Project Technical Advisors, ASEM AML Project Technical Advisor's Report and Recommendations, September 2003 distributed by UNODC.

ASEM, External Relation http://europa.eu.int/comm/external_relations/asem/intro/ Bank of Thailand Act B.E. 2485 (1942).

Basel Committee on Banking Supervision, Core Principles for Effective Banking Supervision, 1977.

Basel Committee on Banking Supervision, Customer Due Diligence for Banks, October. 2001.

Basel Committee on Banking Supervision, Core Principles Methodology, October 2006.

Baer, D. (2016). Shell companies hide about $1 trillion taken from poor countries every year. Business Insider, April 4. Retrieved September 5, 2019. http://www.businessinsider. com/shell–companies–hide–developing–world–moneyl–2016–4.

Baker, S. and Shorrock, E. (2009). Gatekeepers, corporate structures, and their role in money laundering. Tracing Stolen Assets: A Practitioner's Handbook.

Basel Institute on Governance: Basel, Switzerland.

Ball, J. (2012). Offshore secrets: How many companies do 'sham directors' control? The Guardian, November 26. Retrieved on September 6, 2019. http://www.theguardian. com/uk/datablog/2012/nov/26/offshore–secrets–companies–sham–directors.

Baradaran, S., Findley, M., Nielson, D. and Sharman, J. (2014). Funding terror. University of Pennsylvania Law Review, 162, 477–536.

Benner, Katie. "U.S. Accuses 33 of Laundering Billions to Fund North Korea Weapons." The New York Times International, 29 May 2020, A15. Print.

Berbey de Rojas, D. (2008). Panama: The role of the protector in the private interest foundation. Trusts & Trustees, 14(5), 350–353.

Biedermann, M. (2015). G8 principles: Identifying the anonymous. Brigham Young University International Law & Management Review, 11, 72–92.

Boles, J. (2015). Financial sector executives as targets for money laundering liability. American Business Law Journal, 52, 365–433.

Boschini, F.D. (2006). Private foundations and reserved powers trusts. Trusts & Estates, 145, 46–50.

BIS. History of Basel Committee and its membership http://www.bis.org/bcbs/history.htm.

BIS, About the Basel Committee http://www.bis.org/bcbs/history.htm.

BOT, Bank of Thailand News.

BOT, Financial Sector Assessment Program, http://www.bot.or.th/BoThomepage/BankAtWork/Financial_Supervision/FSAP/ FSAPindex.asp

Broome, J., Anti-Money Laundering: International Practice and Policies. Hong Kong.

Browning, L., Davison, L., Basu, K. and Lee, R. (2018). Hill briefs: US second largest tax haven. BNA Daily Tax Report, January 31.

Cao, L. (2004). The transnational and sub–national in global crimes. Berkeley Journal of International Law, 22, 59–97.

Carr, K. and Grow, B. (2011). Special report: A little house of secrets on the great plains. Reuters, June 28. Retrieved on September 14, 2019. ://www.reuters.com/article/us–usa–shell–companies.

Christensen, J. (2012). The hidden trillions: Secrecy, corruption, and the offshore interface. Crime, Law, and Social Change, 57(3), 325–343.

Compin, F. (2008). The role of accounting in money laundering and money dirtying. Critical Perspectives in Accounting 19, 591–602.

Crandall, D., Backstrom, L., Cosley, D., Suri, D., Huttenlocher, D. and Kleinberg, J. (2010). Inferring social ties from geographic coincidences. Proceedings of the National Academy of Sciences, 107(52), 22436–22441.

Crumbley, D.L, Fenton, E., and Smith, S. (2019). Forensic and Investigative Accounting. Chicago: Wolters Kluwer, Chapter 7.

CIA, The World Fact Book https://www.cia.gov/cia/publications/factbook/ geos/th.html.

CICAD, Inter American Drug Abuse Control Commission http://www.cicad.oas.org/en/default.asp.

Civil and Commercial Code Books I to VI. 462.

Civil Procedure Code B.E. 2477 (1943).

Commercial Banking Act 1962.

Corporate Governance Sub-Committee on Commercial Banks, Financial Companies.

Editorial: Tackling human trade forcefully, Bangkok Post, 31-03-07.

Editorial: A serious and sensitive issue, Bangkok Post, 10-10-07.

Editorial: NLA no longer has a mandate, Bangkok Post, 15-12-07.

Egmont Group, Statement of Purpose of the Egmont Group of Financial Intelligence Units, Guernsey, 23 June 2004.

Egmont Group, Information Paper on Financial Intelligence Units and the Egmont Group. www.egmontgroup.org/info_paper_final_092003.pdf.

English Language Law Forum, February 17, 1999 http://www.thailawforum.com/articles/moneylaunderingtg.html.

68

Extradition Act B.E. 2472 (1929).

Europe Publishing, 2004.

FATF, The Forty Recommendations, 2004.

FATF, Nine Special Recommendations, 22 October 2004.

FATF, Combating the abuse of Non-Profit Organizations: International Practices, October 2002.

FATF, FATF 2004-2005 Annual Report, http://www.oecd.org/dataoecd/41/25/3498062.pdf.

FATF-GAFI, What is the FATF?, http://www.fatf-gafi.org/document/57/0,3343,en 32250379 32235720 34432121 _1_1_1,00.html.

FATF, Non-Cooperative Countries and Territories, www.fatf-gafi.org/document/4/0,2340,en 32250379 _32236992_33916420_1_1_1_1,00.html.

Financial Action Task Force (2004), "Money Laundering and Terrorist Financing Trends and Indicators: Initial Perspectives", Money Laundering and Terrorist Financing Typologies 2004-2005, June 2005.

Financial Action Task Force (2006), Background Documents – Summaries of Trade-Based Money Laundering Case Studies and Domestic Regimes, FATF Secure Website.

Financial Action Task Force (2006), Background Documents – Summary of Responses to Trade-Based Money Laundering Questionnaire, FATF Secure Website.

Fisman, R. and Shang-Jin Wei (2001), "Tax Rates and Tax Evasion: Evidence from "Missing Imports" in China", National Bureau of Economic Research Working Paper 8551, October 2001.

Goetzl, A. (2005), "Why Don't Trade Numbers Add Up?" ITTO (International Tropical Timber Organization) Tropical Forest Update 15/1 2005.

Gilmore, W.C., Dirty Money, The evolution of international measures to counter Money.

Gulati (1987), "A Note on Trade Mis invoicing", in Capital Flight and Third World Debt, Lessard, Donald and John Williamson (eds.), Washington DC: Institute for International Economics, pp. 68-78.

HM Treasury, Financial Stability, the Financial Sector Assessment Program (FSAP). http://www.hm-treasury.gov.uk/documents/financial_services/fin_stability/fin_finstability_fsap.cfm463.

Hon. Suchart Traiprasit – Attorney General of Thailand, The Role of Thai Prosecutors in the Fight against the Transnational Crime.

IAIS, Annual Report 2006–2007, http://www.iaisweb.org/__temp/2006-2007_Annual_report.pdf.

IAIS, Insurance Core Principles and Methodology, 2003 http://www.insurance.gov.gy/Documents/IAIS%20Core%20Principles.pdf.

IAIS, Insurance Principles, Standards and Guidance Paper, November 2005 http://www. iaisweb.org/133_ENU_HTML.asp.

IAIS, Anti-Money Laundering Guidance Notes for Insurance Supervisors and Insurance Entities, January 2002.

ICSA, About ICSA http://www.icsa.bz/html/history.html.

IMF Legal Team, IMF Legal Team's Report on AML-CFT, Thailand, September 2005.

IMF Technical Team, IMF Technical Team's Report on AML-CFT, Thailand, April 2006.

IMF, Detailed Assessment Questionnaire – Anti-Money Laundering and Combating the Financing of Terrorism, Thailand, February 2007.

IMF – Legal Department, Thailand: Detailed Assessment Report on Anti-Money Laundering and Combating the Financing of Terrorism, July 24 2007, (Draft).

IMF – Legal Department, Thailand: Detailed Assessment Report on Anti-Money Laundering and Combating the Financing of Terrorism, July 24 2007.

IMF and World Bank (approved by Mark Allen and Denny Leipziger), The standards and codes initiatives – Is it effective? And how can it be improved, 2005 http://www.imf. org/external/np/pp/eng/2005/070105a.pdf.

IMF and World Bank, Anti- Money Laundering and Combating the Financing of Terrorism: Observations Going Forward, Supplementary Information, 2005 http:// www.imf.org/external/np/pp/eng/2005/083105.pdf.

IMF and World Bank, Intensified Work on AML-CFT, 17 April 2002 http://www.imf. org/external/np/mae/aml/2002/eng/091002.htm.

IMOLIN (International Money Laundering Information Network), United Nations Global Program against Money Laundering.

International Affairs Department - Office of the Attorney General. Laws Related to Mutual Legal Assistance in Criminal Matters, fifth edition: 2005.

International Program – UK Charity Commission, UK Charity Commission's Report on Thailand's NGO Regime, January 2007.

Inventory of International Nonproliferation Organizations and Regimes – Center for Nonproliferation Studies, International Convention for the Suppression of the Financing of Terrorism, 2006.

IOSCO, Objectives and Principles of Securities Regulations, May 2003, http://www. apgml.org/documents/docs/15/IOSCO%20Principles.pdf.

Laws and Regulations, http://www.thailand.com/exports/html/law_general_09.htm.

Lyman, David (Senior Partner Tilleke & Gibbins Rev.), Money Laundering, Thailand.

Measures for Anti-Money Laundering and Combating the Financing of Terrorism: Policy Statement on International Cooperation.

Ministry of Justice (Thailand), Thailand Country Report: Synergies and Responses: Strategic Alliances in Crime Prevention and Criminal Justice, the Eleventh United Nations Congress on Crime Prevention and Criminal Justice, Thailand, 18 – 25 April 2005.

NCGC, Order No. 1/2545, 30 April 2002.

Nemes, Irene & Coss, Graeme, Effective Legal Research, second edition, Australia: Butterworths, 2001.

News report: Government amends AMLO structure, Bangkok Post, 28 February 2007.

News report: Thailand slips down the list, now seen as more corrupt, Bangkok Post, 27 September 2007.

News report on business section: New rules aim to detect money laundering, Bangkok Post, 29 October 2007.

News report: Bill creates 7 new offences, Bangkok Post, 15 November 2007.

News report: Sonthi: Separatist movements part of int'l terror network, by Wassana Nanuam, Bangkok Post, 21 November 2007 465.

News report: Thaksin faces up to 26 years in jail, Bangkok Post, 27 November 2007.

News report: DSI officers suspended over expenses claims, Bangkok Post, 7 December 2007.

News report: B 16 m cash brought in through airport still here, says AMLO, by Thanida Tansubhapol, Bangkok Post 13 December 2007.

Non-Cooperative Countries and Territories http://www.fatf-gafi.org/document/4/0,2340,en_32250379_32236992_33916420_1_1_1_1,00.html.

OICV-IOSCO, General Information on IOSCO, http://www.iosco.org/about/

OICV-IOSCO IOSCO Historical Background, http://www.iosco.org/about/

Paper (2). Case Studies on the Links between Organized Crime Groups in Asia and Europe, 2005.

Pacific Finance Association (APFA) annual conference, Bangkok, July 2001 http://pioneer.netserv.chula.ac.th/~ppasuk/goodgovernancethailandsexperience.doc.

Penal Code B.E. 2499 (1956).

Phasook Pongpaichit and Rangsit Piriyarangsan (Faculty of Economics of Chulalongkorn University), Lottery, Brothel, Gambling House, Amphetamine, Illegal Economy and Public Policy in Thailand" 1996.

Phasuk Phongpaichit, Good Governance: Thailand's Experience – Paper for Asia

Proposed Amendment to AMLA Considered by the Council of State – No. 415/2550, 2007.

Public Procurement in Asia and the Pacific Progress and Challenges in 25 Countries, Thematic Review Special Case Investigation Act 2004.

TBA, TBA's AML-CFT Policy, 5 August 2005.

TBA, Guidelines on Know Your Customers (KYC) and Customer Due Diligence (CDD) to meet international standards related to financial transactions, 2007.

Thailand Jurisdiction Report (2004 – 2005) to APG Annual Meeting.

Thailand Jurisdiction Report (2005 – 2006) to APG Annual Meeting.

UN, (Asia and Far East Institute for the Prevention of Crime and the Treatment of Offenders, Ekobrottsmyndigheten Swedish National Economic Crimes Bureau, Report of the Workshop Measures to Combat Economic Crime, Including Money –Laundering – Eleventh United Nations Congress on Crime Prevention and Criminal Justice, Bangkok, 18- 25 April 2005, Tokyo, Japan, February 2006.

UN, The United Nations Convention against Illicit Traffic in Narcotic Drugs and Psychotropic Substances, 1988 (1988 Vienna Convention).

UN, International Convention for the Suppression of the Financing of Terrorism, 1999 (Convention against FT or Terrorist Financing Convention).

UN, The United Nations Convention against Transnational Organized Crime, 2000 (Palermo Convention).

UN, The United Nations Convention against Corruption, 2003.

UN Information Service, United Nations Convention against Corruption, (Fact sheet).

UNIS/CP/484 http://www.unis.unvienna.org/unis/pressrels/2004/uniscp484.html, 10 May 2004.

UN, The United Nations Convention against Illicit Traffic in Narcotic Drugs and Psychotropic Substances, 1988 (Status of the Convention) www.unodc.org/pdf/treaty_adherence_convention_1988.pdf.

United States – Department of the Treasury (Office of Foreign Assets Control) http://www.treasury.gov/offices/enforcement/ofac/programs.

UNODC –Terrorism Prevention Branch, Comparative Study on Anti-Terrorism

Legislative Developments in Asian and Pacific Countries: Cambodia, Indonesia, Lao People's Democratic Republic, Malaysia, the Philippines, Timor-Leste and Viet Nam, Vienna, January 2006.

UNODC. Definitions of terrorism http://www.unodc.org/unodc/terrorism_definitions.html.

UNODC, Signatories to the UN Convention against Transnational Crime and its Protocols http://www.unodc.org/unodc/crime_cicp_signatures.html.

UNODC, Legislative Guide to the Universal Anti-Terrorism Conventions and Protocols, 2004 http://www.unodc.org/pdf/Legislative%20Guide%20Mike% 2006-56981_E_Ebook.pdf .

US – Department of State (the Bureau of International Narcotics and Law Enforcement Affairs), The International Narcotics Control Strategy Report, 2004 http://www.state.gov/p/inl/rls/nrcrpt/2003/vol2/html/29910.htm.

Wolfsberg Group, Global Banks: Global Standards http://www.wolfsberg- principles.com/

World Bank Group (Mark Butler, FSEFI), Aide-Memoire – Anti-Money Laundering and Combating the Financing of Terrorism--the Kingdom of Thailand, April 21 – 27, 2006.

World Bank, World Bank's Aide-Memoire on AML-CFT, Thailand, April 2006.

ABOUT THE AUTHOR

A renowned Financial Security Expert, a Doctoral product, SBS Swiss Business School, Zurich, Switzerland of Business Administration, Master of Applied Business Research, Master of Business Administration, and an Executive MBA candidate of Cybersecurity at Ottawa University in the United States of America. I have acquired two (2) decades of specialization in financial planning and advisory, risk management and cybersecurity.

Over the period, I have had experiences in financial greenfield projects, working with various institutions and stakeholders in more than a dozen countries across Africa and Latin America, to improve access and quality of financial products and services for low-income and underserved individuals.

I have held Senior leadership positions in Investment Companies, Microfinance Banks, Savings and Loans companies, and Social Enterprises, where I have led teams, projects, and initiatives to expand market reach through greenfield projects, developed new products, deployed alternative delivery channels, developed public-private partnerships for national inclusive programs, and conducted consultancy projects for UNCDF related to donor funding projects. I have also provided technical and operational support and advice to regional and global networks and partners.

At the helm of FINCA – USA (Nigeria subsidiary) as CEO, and as an influential figure within ACCION International, USA, I demonstrated prowess in international development initiatives. My endeavors in these institutions were characterized by the cultivation of substantial social capital, extending both quantitatively and qualitatively.

I am passionate about availing my two decades of experience in corporate governance to industry and academia to enhance longitudinal exposure to developmental trends beneficial to multinational public and private sectors, to make our world a better place.

Printed in the United States
by Baker & Taylor Publisher Services